CW00548922

Making Workshops Work

Communicators. The most important management skill is communication. The authors of this series are all specialists in the art.

Blank Page To First Draft In 15 Minutes
The most effective shortcut to preparing a speech or presentation
Phillip Khan-Panni

2-4-6-8 How Do You Communicate?
How to make your point in just a minute
Philip Khan-Panni

'Philip Khan-Panni "knows what he knows", expresses it clearly, cleverly and concisely. A must read.'
JIM RHODE, CSP, PRESIDENT NATIONAL SPEAKERS ASSOCIATION, USA

Communicate with Emotional Intelligence
Use personal competencies and key relationship skills to influence others and get results
John Eaton & Roy Johnson

Resolving Conflict
Establish trusting and productive relationships in the workplace
Shay & Magaret McConnon

Communicators is an imprint of How To Books.
For further details please send for a free copy of the latest catalogue
3 Newtec Place, Magdalen Road, Oxford OX4 1RE, United Kingdom.

Making Workshops Work

Ensure your workshops create high-octane interaction

Dr Rob Yeung

communicators

Published by How To Books Ltd,
3 Newtec Place, Magdalen Road,
Oxford OX4 1RE, United Kingdom.
Tel: (01865) 793806. Fax: (01865) 248780
email: info@howtobooks.co.uk
http://www.howtobooks.co.uk

All rights reserved. No part of this work may be reproduced
or stored in an information retrieval system (other than for
purposes of review) without the express permission of the publisher in writing.

© Copyright 2002 Dr Rob Yeung

First edition 2002

British Library Cataloguing in Publication Data.
A catalogue record for this book is available from the British Library.

Edited by Diana Brueton
Cover design by Baseline Arts Ltd, Oxford

Produced for How To Books by Deer Park Productions
Typeset by Kestrel Data, Exeter
Printed and bound by Bell & Bain Ltd, Glasgow

NOTE: The material contained in this book is set out in good faith for general
guidance and no liability can be accepted for loss or expense incurred as a
result of relying in particular circumstances on statements made in this book.
Laws and regulations are complex and liable to change, and readers should
check the current position with the relevant authorities before making
personal arrangements.

Communicators is an imprint of How To Books.

Contents

Preface   **7**

**1 Getting to Grips with
    Facilitation**   **9**

Facilitation benefits you, the people around you,
your organisation and your customers. And it can
help with a surprisingly large range of problems and
issues.

2 Setting an Agenda   **21**

Facilitation isn't just about doing a good job on the
day – half of the work is in the preparation and the
little things.

**3 Getting the Basics of
    Facilitation Right**   **36**

Facilitation is all about asking the right questions,
listening and probing ever deeper with increasingly
insightful questions. And here's how you do it.

**4 Kicking Off on the Right
    Foot**   **48**

Setting the scene is critical if you want to do a good
job.

**5 Livening Things Up with
    Tools and Techniques**   **62**

The basic tools and techniques in this chapter will
help you to structure a workshop or meeting for
everyone's benefit.

6   Injecting Energy into Meetings and Workshops   **73**

Learning to look after the group dynamic will help you keep a group interested and on course for delivering a good result.

7   Dealing with Difficult People   **84**

People who talk too much and people who talk too little. Here's how to deal with them both – and many more types besides.

8   Handling Sticky Situations   **96**

When arguments get out of hand, use these pointers to defuse conflict and get the group talking constructively again.

9   Building Up Your Repertoire of Tools and Techniques   **103**

Using the proven tools in this chapter will help you to facilitate even more topics.

10   Making Decisions   **117**

Talking is great, but at the end of the day you have to agree on next steps. These techniques will ensure your group makes the right decision.

11   Leading Your Group Over the Finish Line   **124**

The best laid plans can go wrong! So here's how to get the group on track again to a great result.

12   Taking Facilitation to the Next Level   **133**

Facilitation doesn't stop when your group leaves the room. Here's how to turn yourself into a first-class facilitator.

Preface

Hands up if you think that your meetings are 100% as effective, efficient and enjoyable as you would like them to be. It's a question that I have asked hundreds of people over the years on dozens of facilitation skills training workshops. Unsurprisingly, no one has ever put their hand up.

The sad truth is that people don't use meetings effectively. Sometimes we have meetings that seem to have no purpose. We argue and we talk over each other, while some people seem to contribute nothing at all. Or one person will talk and talk and send everyone else to sleep. Who hasn't been in a meeting where they have been watching the clock and thinking about something better they could be doing?

But it doesn't have to be like that at all. There is a world of tools and techniques to capture people's imaginations, inject creativity and enjoyment into the mix, and still achieve your goals. It will help you to generate fresh ideas, steer people through conflict and disagreements, and turn ideas into reality. And, with change management being such a hot topic in business today, if you want to get involved in making change happen, making workshops work is a key skill for you too.

So why not design a workshop to channel people's thinking to tackle a tricky problem? Or use a fast-paced and frenetic focus group to gather information and ideas from people rather than have them sitting around talking dryly about a topic?

Facilitation is all about helping people harness their energy and thinking to achieve results. So if you want practical techniques for making workshops work by generating ideas, solving problems and getting people to commit to action, then this book is for you.

Rob Yeung

Chapter 1

Getting to Grips with Facilitation

In this chapter:

♦ **why bother with this 'facilitation' thing?**
♦ **when could you run a workshop?**
♦ **situations you definitely should not facilitate**
♦ **what does successful facilitation look like?**
♦ **facilitation is not the same as being everybody's friend**
♦ **what is the difference between a workshop and a focus group?**
♦ **what's in it for you?**

In today's busy and increasingly competitive world, we all want more. We want things to be faster, sexier, brighter, quicker, cheaper and better quality. So why not expect the same from the many sorts of meetings that we attend?

Growing numbers of people are finding that workshops can help to achieve all of these things. In fact, whether it's a workshop or focus group, a brainstorming session or continuous improvement group, or perhaps a team or project meeting, they can all benefit from the principle of running workshops —

and *facilitation is the skill you need to make workshops work*. Facilitation is about designing and running workshops, but it is not the same as lecturing or teaching. It is about getting participants engaged in talking to you and each other to get the best out of everybody.

There is no big secret to facilitation. It begins with planning and preparing for a meeting, then steering people through a process to help them to achieve whatever the purpose of the meeting is. And whether you are a member of the group or team, perhaps the team's manager, or even an external consultant, facilitation will help you achieve your goals.

Doesn't that sound like something worth doing?

Facilitation can help you get what you want

Facilitation benefits everyone. You can help a group of people achieve the aims of a meeting, workshop or focus group *more quickly*. Rather than letting the topic of discussion wander randomly, you as the facilitator are steering people to keep them on track to meet the aims of the meeting.

There are other benefits for the group too. By facilitating a workshop or meeting, you could expect to:

♦ Help participants get more involved in meetings to keep them awake and productive.

- Draw more innovative ideas out of them.
- Resolve conflict between groups of people with different views.
- Get more 'buy-in' to decisions because participants have come up with the ideas themselves rather than those decisions being put upon them.
- Develop the thinking and skills of the people in your meetings.
- Inject a bit of life into otherwise dull meetings.

What exactly does the facilitator do?

The facilitator's first task is to help a group of people decide on the **objectives** for the meeting or workshop. Sometimes a sponsor – a person outside of the group itself – sets the objectives, and sometimes the group agrees the objectives. Whichever the case, once the facilitator has identified these, *the facilitator's job is to help the group meet those objectives*.

Rather than telling people how to meet those objectives, the facilitator's job is to *help the group to come up with their own ideas* for how to meet them. Instead of lecturing or presenting to them, a facilitator tries to set the agenda and ask the right questions to get people thinking.

You can use facilitation in all sorts of scrapes and situations

You can facilitate almost any meeting where you want to waste less time going in circles around an issue, and more time tackling the topic head on and agreeing on what to actually do. But there are some common situations where it can be a good idea to have a facilitator to guide the structure of a meeting.

Some of these situations are around gathering new ideas or feedback from people. For example:

♦ Brainstorming ideas for a new product.
♦ Finding a solution to a difficult problem such as falling sales, poor customer satisfaction or perhaps delays on a production line.
♦ Conducting a focus group with customers to get feedback on an existing product or service.
♦ Asking employees why they are unhappy or dissatisfied with their jobs.
♦ Organising an employee focus group to get buy-in to a new organisational vision or strategy – perhaps during a 'change management programme'.

Other situations are around handling conflict and disagreements, such as:

♦ Resolving conflict between individuals to break out of a deadlock on a contentious issue.
♦ Helping two or more groups with opposing stances to reach consensus on a way forward.

But facilitation can also be used to develop teams and people's skills, for example:

♦ Building team spirit before starting to work together on a project.

♦ Running a learning or training workshop to develop people's skills.

Facilitation isn't always the answer

Although facilitation is a powerful tool for achieving results, it can't perform miracles. You may also want to avoid facilitation when you need to add your own expert knowledge. Facilitation is about asking questions to help *other* people come up with the answers. A facilitator who talks and adds his or her own ideas isn't facilitating anymore, he or she is lecturing or presenting.

So when you feel that you have particular insights into a topic and want to contribute your ideas and opinions, you may want to set up a non-facilitated meeting to discuss the issue. Or perhaps you could ask someone else to facilitate instead.

Specific situations that do not suit facilitation

♦ **A crisis.** If there was a fire in the building, do you really have time to consult everyone and ask them how they want to handle it? You just need to find the nearest fire exit and leave! Similarly, when things go wrong in the workplace, you may not have the time to get input from everyone and make sure they all feel comfortable with the course of action. Especially if you're the team's manager, you may need to bark orders at people and handle the problem as quickly as possible. After the crisis it may be appropriate to facilitate a session to talk about how well or badly you handled the crisis, why the problem arose in the first place and how to prevent it from happening again.

♦ **For tackling everyday problems.** There is such a thing as overkill. When it's a straightforward decision you don't want to have to ask everyone for their opinions. If most people seem to be in agreement, why waste time designing a workshop and asking everyone how they feel about it? Just let them get on with it instead!

Successful facilitation focuses on three vital elements

It is time to introduce just a little jargon. To achieve the group's objectives a facilitator needs to pay attention to **content**, **process**, and **group dynamics**:

1 Content

The 'content' element of facilitation is the subject matter that the group is working on. It is the topics and issues that they discuss – it is *what the group wants or needs to achieve*.

So it is quite easy to figure out what the content is. You just need to ask yourself: 'What are we trying to achieve?' Your answer might be something along the lines of 'Finding a way to increase company cash flow' or 'Discovering new ideas to reduce our company's impact on the environment'.

In most meetings we focus only on the content. We talk and we talk about what we need to do. But just focusing on content is rarely the most efficient or effective way of getting what the group wants.

2 Process

Good facilitators help the discussion to progress, allowing the content to emerge – without actually contributing to the content themselves. The facilitator's role is therefore to control the 'process' – *how the meeting will take place*.

As the facilitator, you need to design a process – a framework or structure – to help steer the discussion during a meeting or workshop. Just a few elements of this structure include:

♦ How long the workshop or focus group will last.
♦ Whether to use any exercises or activities incorporating tools or techniques (such as those in Chapters 5 and 6) to help the discussion along.
♦ Where the meeting will be held.
♦ How to handle conflict between individuals who may disagree.
♦ The order in which you discuss various topics.

In fact, about half of this book focuses on equipping you to design a process to move a group discussion forward until the participants achieve their aims.

3 Group dynamics

Dynamics describe the interactions that you can see between people in the group. These interactions are a reflection of the climate – *how people are feeling*. It may sound obvious that it's important to pay attention to how people are feeling – whether they are tired or bored, angry or distracted. But you would be amazed at how many people design a fantastic process and keep a close eye on the content and yet ignore the tell-tale signs of how people are feeling.

It is critical that you pay attention to the group dynamics and check that they are appropriate for your group. By focusing only on the process and content, you might miss problems such as areas of conflict or negative emotions within the group. These kinds of problems could mean that the discussion might drag on and fall behind schedule. Or a dominant person – perhaps because they are very senior or just a bully – in the group could stifle open discussion. At worst, if you focus only on process and content, you could end up bullying your group into accepting a solution or end result with which no one (apart from you) actually agrees.

Facilitation isn't just about being 'touchy feely'

When asked about facilitation, a lot of people actually throw their hands up in horror – they associate it with a particular 'touchy feely' style that *some* facilitators can use. At its worst, a facilitator who uses this style might:

- ◆ Nurture and support the group.
- ◆ Try to become a universally-liked friend to the participants.
- ◆ Be passive and not dare to interrupt or disagree with the group.
- ◆ Even engage in 'psycho-babble' and treat facilitation as a solution for every single problem that people face both in work and outside of it.

In a phrase, it's a 'chat show host' style of facilitation – being terribly earnest and supportive, but perhaps not as driven as necessary for solving problems in the workplace. Unfortunately, this style has given the very word 'facilitation' a bad reputation.

Driving for results through facilitation

The 'touchy feely' style of facilitation may be appropriate in some limited situations – such as a training and development workshop. However, if you need to deliver results, it may be more appropriate to adopt a more investigative style of facilitation.

A facilitator who actually wants to deliver results (as opposed to just make everyone 'feel happy') will tend to:

- ◆ Support the group only as appropriate, but push them to work hard when necessary.
- ◆ Be more focused on achieving results than being a friend to the participants.
- ◆ Disagree with participants if he/she feels that a valid point needs to be made.

♦ Treat facilitation only as a tool that can be helpful in many of the situations that people face at work.

So if any of your colleagues/clients/customers/sponsors question you about the value of facilitation, just explain to them the difference between the merely 'touchy feely' style as compared with the tougher style that this book advocates in order to achieve results with groups.

Don't worry about what you call your meetings

There are lots of names for the get-togethers that we facilitate – '**workshop**', '**meeting**', '**session**' and '**focus group**' just as a few examples. There are no strict definitions for these labels. However, some people (but not all) do tend to think about them in certain ways. Typically:

♦ The phrase 'focus group' tends to be used when a group is called together to generate ideas or discuss what they do or don't like about something, for example a new product, an existing service, or the organisation that employs them.
♦ The label 'workshop' is more often used when a group is asked to debate and resolve an issue.

In this book I use these words and phrases synonymously because people in the real world use them interchangeably. You can call it whatever you like – as long as you think the term captures the essence of what the group is trying to achieve. You could call a **brainstorming session** an 'imagination creativity session' or just simply a '**meeting**'. The labels matter less than the fact that you must manage process, content and group dynamics to help a group achieve their objectives.

Facilitation benefits *you*

We have talked about the benefits of facilitation and a little bit about what it actually entails. But what's in it for *you*?

Here are just a few reasons why it's worth your time to master the art of facilitation:

♦ You will be recognised by your colleagues as someone who can get meetings moving along more quickly. Your colleagues will come to you to help them resolve disagreement and get results faster.
♦ Organisations are increasingly obsessed with change management. Making change happen often requires people to facilitate workshops to help people within the organisation understand the need for change and the role that each individual will play in the overall change.
♦ If you ever want to enter (or currently work in) management consultancy, facilitation is a prized skill. It is vital to be able to facilitate a sales meeting with a new client to help them understand how you can help them. And, once you have started working with them, you may need to facilitate

focus groups to discover what's wrong in the client's organisation, and then run workshops with the client to agree how to fix it all.

If you can develop a reputation for good facilitation skills, promotion or a new job can't be far away.

In summary . . .

♦ **Facilitation helps people get results from meetings more quickly and more enjoyably.**

♦ **You can facilitate almost any sort of meeting – apart from when there's a crisis or the problem is so mundane that facilitation would just be a waste of time.**

♦ **As the facilitator, part of your role is to design an effective process.**

♦ **Your group is responsible for coming up with the content of the discussion.**

♦ **But you are also responsible for watching the group dynamics.**

♦ **Don't worry whether a meeting is called a 'focus group', 'workshop' or anything else – the principles of designing and delivering them are the same.**

♦ **Learning to facilitate well will turn you into a prized and valuable asset.**

Chapter 2

Setting an Agenda

In this chapter:

♦ **why research matters**
♦ **preparing materials before a workshop**
♦ **setting homework for your participants**
♦ **why lunch shouldn't matter (but does)**
♦ **capturing ideas**
♦ **handling a bit of nerves**

Designing an effective process takes time. You need to think about what you want to achieve, who should be invited to participate, and how you are going to introduce the workshop and start to get people talking.

How long should you expect to spend in preparing for a workshop?

Unfortunately, it's like asking how long a piece of string is. It all depends on how tricky the discussion is going to be. If, for instance, you are running a routine team meeting, you may only need half an hour to write up an agenda. For tough workshops – perhaps on sensitive topics or where you may not have met the participants before – as a rule of thumb *it's worth investing twice as long preparing for a workshop as you would do in running it.*

Research creates the foundation for your workshop

Research serves a number of purposes. Firstly, it will help you to identify clear objectives for the workshop and think about the tools or techniques you can use to help the group meet those objectives.

Secondly, it will help you to understand the context underlying the need for the workshop in the first place.

Equally importantly though, *doing a little research with the participants will help you to start building a rapport with them*. Otherwise, if you turn up at the workshop never having met the participants, they could be a bit hesitant and wary of you – after all you're practically a complete stranger. This is especially important if you are an external consultant, brought in to help a particular group.

There are two steps for researching before a workshop.

1 Talk to the project sponsor

If someone (or some people) has asked you to set up and facilitate the workshop, you need to book an appointment with them to ask them why they want the workshop in the first place.

You need to think about the questions that you can ask. For example, not all of the following questions may be appropriate! Some questions to ask might include:

♦ 'Why do you want me to run this workshop/focus group/session?'
♦ 'What is the purpose of the workshop? What are its objectives?'
♦ 'Who will attend the workshop? What do they each do? And why have they been invited?' A little about their job titles, experience and background will help you to understand the individual participants better.
♦ 'Are there any political issues or conflicts that I should be aware of?'
♦ 'Is there any hidden agenda to the workshop at all?'
♦ 'Are there any constraints – for example location, timing, or cost – for running the workshop that I should be aware of?'
♦ 'What would you consider a satisfactory outcome for the workshop?'

You should also ask what outputs the sponsor would like from the workshop. Do they want a transcript of the comments made in the workshop? Perhaps a lengthy report or maybe just an executive summary of the results?

If you are running a meeting or workshop for your own team, you are the project sponsor – but you would still need to think about the above questions to clarify in your own mind why and how to run it.

2 Talk to the participants

If you are running a workshop with people you don't
know very well, you should ideally try to get some
time with each and every one of the participants. Even
if you can't meet them face-to-face, at least try to get
them on the telephone for just a few minutes.

Most critically, it is worth checking that everyone has
the same information. Assumptions can be a real killer
if they are wrong! For example:

♦ Do the participants know that they have been
   invited (or told to attend) the workshop or
   meeting? Do they know the time/date/place of the
   workshop or meeting? It's not uncommon for a
   facilitator to assume that the sponsor has told the
   participants all of those details – and for the
   sponsor to assume that the facilitator will sort those
   details out!
♦ Do they know who you are? If not, it's worth
   spending thirty seconds introducing yourself – just
   to break the ice a little bit.
♦ Do the participants know the purpose/objectives of
   the workshop?

If you can, it's also worth getting some input from the
participants on the process you are planning for the
workshop:

♦ 'What would *you* like to get out of this workshop?'
♦ 'Are there any issues in the team/group of which I
   should be aware?' Here, you are looking for

information such as 'Oh, David has just been given a formal written warning for underperformance' or 'Off the record, Simon and Brian don't really get on with each other because . . .'

It is never going to be possible to provide you, the reader, with an exhaustive list of questions for doing your research. It's up to you to think about what you need for facilitating your meeting successfully.

Preparing your materials will take the pressure off you

There could be up to dozens of pairs of eyes watching your every move during a workshop. So why not take the pressure off by preparing some materials for the participants to look at instead?

Some questions for you to think about:

Slides or overhead transparencies

If you need to present any information to the group, are you going to use any slides or overhead transparencies in the meeting? Remember that these can often take quite a lot of time to prepare – especially if you need someone else's help in using software such as PowerPoint.

Flipchart notes

What (if anything) are you going to write up on a flipchart beforehand? For example, would it be helpful to write up the objectives of the meeting beforehand?

Handouts

Are you going to give anything to people during the meeting (for them to read while you are talking) or after it? Some common handouts include:

♦ A copy of the agenda for the meeting.
♦ A workbook – perhaps filled with questionnaires, titbits of information. These are particularly useful if you are facilitating a training workshop aimed at helping people identify what they need to do in order to develop their skills.
♦ A copy of any slides or overhead transparencies that you might be using.
♦ If you have never met the group before (for example you are an external consultant), you may want to include a short précis of your background and relevant experience in facilitating similar groups.

Your briefcase

Although many meeting rooms or other venues provide stationery and other essential items, it is often worth preparing your own kit bag. Otherwise, it can be amazing how much time can be wasted trying to find some masking tape or Post-It notes. You don't want to give your participants even the slightest feeling that you are an inept and unprepared facilitator.

Items to take with you might include:

♦ Blu tack or masking tape for fixing flip chart sheets up on walls.
♦ Thick, solvent-free marker pens. If you are writing

up on white boards, make sure that they are
non-permanent and erasable.
♦ Post-It notes.

Think back to other workshops or group sessions in
which you have participated. What materials have
helped to make a meeting run more smoothly?

Introduce 'homework' to make the most of a workshop

People today are busy. We all have too much to do. So
time may be limited for sitting in a workshop. Even
more so when your participants are travelling from all
over the country to attend the meeting. So 'homework'
may be a good way of making the most of that limited
face-to-face time.

Rather than waste time during the workshop
presenting new facts and information to them, why
not give it to the participants beforehand?

However, in order to make it as effective as possible,
do try to:

♦ Keep it short. Busy people are prone to
forgetfulness and/or laziness. The longer the task,
the less likely that the participants will do it.
♦ Send out your materials and then check that all of
the participants have received it. Participants do
sometimes arrive at workshops and claim that they
never received the materials. Sometimes materials

will get sent to the wrong office and sometimes it's an excuse because they forgot or couldn't be bothered. Either way, if you don't check it's easier for them to avoid doing the preparation.

♦ Make the homework as interesting as possible. Rather than just sending them reading material, would it be possible to send out a short questionnaire? Or what about a speech to prepare or a short video to watch?

The little things often matter as much as the big

The physical environment is surprisingly important when it comes to whatever workshop you might be running. Decisions about the location and setting of the meeting room may need to be made days or even weeks in advance – especially if you need to book, for example, an external conference centre.

Venue

Are you going to hold your workshop or meeting in an empty office that happens to be free? Or are you going to book a lavish hotel in the countryside? An important distinction is whether you are going to hold your workshop **on-site** or **off-site**.

It depends a little on the budget that you have for holding the meeting. Having a meeting on-site costs nothing, but it means that the participants can be more easily disturbed by other colleagues, 'urgent' phone calls or messages.

Holding a workshop off-site frees participants up from such day-to-day interruptions. Also getting them away from their familiar office surroundings might allow them to be a little more creative, but you will need to think of issues such as how the participants will travel to the off-site location. And, of course, hiring a conference room has a cost attached to it.

You don't necessarily have to spend a fortune hiring an expensive conference venue for an off-site workshop. For example, I can honestly say that one of the most productive brainstorming sessions I've ever had was late one evening in a pub with colleagues, scribbling on the back of a till receipt with a borrowed pen!

The room

The seating plan can be an important part of the physical environment. The typical office meeting room is set up with a table in the middle of the room with chairs around it. This 'board room' style may be fine for a short, routine meeting – but may not be so good for lengthier workshops.

The most common set-up for a facilitated meeting is to have the tables set up in the shape of a U in the room, with chairs behind the U so that everyone looks inwards towards the centre of the U. Very importantly, this allows you, as the facilitator, to make **eye contact** with each participant. And it allows them to look at you and any presentation material. The U-formation is often used for groups of up to 12 (or at most 16) participants.

An alternative – particularly for larger groups of say 15 to 30 participants – is to set up a number of smaller round tables, with a group of half a dozen or so participants at each table. This set-up is particularly appropriate if you intend to have sub-groups working on different tasks as part of your workshop (see Chapter 6 on syndicate group working).

Matters of comfort

Just a few other things to think about:

♦ What will the dress code for the workshop be? If you are holding it off-site, would it be appropriate for people to dress casually? Or is formal business attire necessary?
♦ When will you schedule breaks in the day (for people to check their mobile phone or email messages – as well as for 'comfort breaks')?
♦ Who will arrange refreshments during those breaks?
♦ Will you provide lunch during a lengthy workshop?
♦ If the workshop is going to last over a couple of days, who is going to arrange overnight accommodation for the participants?

These points may seem trivial – but you shouldn't discount the huge importance that participants can sometimes attach to such matters. Working on an empty stomach or a full bladder is not conducive to group productivity!

Don't waste ideas once you have them

One last area to think about is how you will capture the ideas that are generated in the discussion. There is no 'right' way of capturing ideas. It really is the case that you should use whatever you feel works best for you.

It is worth your while thinking about how to capture ideas – especially as participants frequently want to receive minutes or notes of the outcomes from the workshop.

Hi-tech methods

♦ **Tape recorder.** If you are keen to capture verbatim comments, this could be the tool for you.
♦ **Video camera.** The favoured tool of the market research facilitator. If you need to analyse participants' faces as well as the actual words that they used, then a camera (possibly hidden behind glass) is ideal.

However, one disadvantage of hi-tech methods is that they can make some participants feel more nervous.

Low-tech methods

♦ **Minutes.** One disadvantage of having one of the participants within the group take minutes is that he or she has to concentrate so hard on taking accurate minutes that they may not be able to contribute fully to the meeting.

♦ **Flip chart (or white board) and marker pen.** Another favoured tool of many facilitators – particularly business psychologists and other management consultants. Although you will never capture all of the comments that are made in the workshop, the notes on the flipchart are visible to all of the participants during the workshop – you could perhaps stick completed flipchart sheets up on the walls. This method also allows you the 'power of the pen' – you can choose not to write a statement down that you do not believe the entire group believes in. For example, if a participant says 'we should spend the money now', rather than writing it down you can ask the group 'does everyone agree that we should spend the money now?' or 'can anyone see any difficulties in spending the money now?'. And then, only when the group has reached agreement on the point, you could write it down.

♦ **Scribe.** An alternative to having you write up comments is to involve a second person (either a colleague of yours or even a participant from within the group itself). The disadvantage is that the scribe may not write up the precise words that you want to capture. I have already mentioned the 'power' of holding the pen. By giving the marker pen to your scribe, he or she may start to write comments up without you having the opportunity to probe the group's statements fully.

A warning

If you do choose a flip chart – whether you write it up yourself or use a scribe – make sure you capture the right words. I once asked a question in a workshop about the facilities in the organisation and a participant replied, 'f***ing rubbish'. I wrote 'rubbish' up on the flip chart, and he corrected me by again saying, 'f***ing rubbish', because he wanted to transmit a much stronger complaint back to management and not just a sanitised comment.

So the point is to make sure that you *check that your participants are happy with the wording* if you aren't sure of exactly what to write up.

Nervous energy can be a good thing

It is natural to feel a little tense before an important meeting or workshop. Indeed, the actor Sir Derek Jacobi, says that he still feels almost crippling stage fright before almost every performance in front of a live audience – but he finds that it gets the adrenaline flowing and helps him to put in a great performance. So it's better to feel a bit nervous rather than be too relaxed or feel complacent and risk doing a bad job of things.

Here are a few tips for handling those 'butterflies in your stomach':

◆ **Rehearse** what you are going to say. Many people find that it helps to rehearse their introductions out loud. An ex-colleague of mine used to take his presentation materials home and rehearse out loud in front of his cat! Do whatever will help you to feel more comfortable.

♦ **Learn to breathe** from your diaphragm. If you can see your stomach rising and falling with each breath, then you are breathing correctly. Physiologists tell us that breathing which makes your chest rise and fall is more likely to make you feel anxious.

♦ **Take breaths between sentences**. When people are nervous, they have a tendency to speak more quickly. A trick for slowing yourself down is to practise taking a pause between sentences. It may feel odd when you are practising, but when you are fired up on the day of the workshop, taking a breath (or pausing to swallow) between sentences will force you to slow down and appear calmer.

♦ **Imagine your participants naked** or sitting on the toilet! This one doesn't work for everyone, but I know plenty of people who have used it and found that it makes them smile and feel more relaxed. When you first look around the room, just picture what each member of the group would look like naked – the absurdity of the idea should bring a smile to your face.

In summary . . .

♦ Research is vital for setting clear objectives.

♦ Don't forget to ask the sponsor(s) what output they want from the workshop.

♦ Talking to the participants before a workshop also helps you to build up a bit of vital rapport.

♦ Prepare handouts or other materials when you need to communicate a lot of information to your workshop participants.

♦ Don't let little things such as forgetting to arrange coffee or lunch disrupt the flow of discussion in your workshop.

♦ Tape recorders and video cameras are great when you need to capture verbatim comments.

♦ Otherwise use a flip chart for capturing the main points of a discussion.

♦ A bit of practice and learning to use psychological techniques can help you manage any nerves.

Chapter 3

Getting the Basics of Facilitation Right

In this chapter:

♦ **learning to ask the right questions**

♦ **using the 'five why' technique**

♦ **the sound of silence and other techniques**

♦ **why can't a facilitator add to the content of the discussion?**

♦ **how can you avoid adding your own opinions?**

♦ **when to command and when to cajole**

We have already established that facilitation is about providing a process for a discussion and monitoring the group dynamics during it, but *not* adding to its content.

You can facilitate even if you know almost nothing about the content of the discussion. The participants may be talking about European employment law, difficulties on the production line, or leading edge IT systems – but that's okay. As a facilitator, you are there to provide a process for the participants to come up with the content themselves.

This chapter covers the skills you need before you start a workshop.

And the key skill during a workshop itself is to be able to ask *insightful questions that challenge the thinking* of the participants in your group.

Questions are the basis of good facilitation

Six simple words form the basis for all of the questions you will need to ask:

♦ What?
♦ How?
♦ Why?
♦ Who?
♦ Where?
♦ When?

Using these six question words forms the entire basis of facilitating a group's thinking. Questions encourage participants in your workshops to generate ideas and explore options.

Question types

There are though a number of ways in which you can construct questions to suit different situations:

♦ **Open questions.** These questions encourage people to express their concerns. Examples include 'What do you think we should do?', 'How could we start to . . . ?', 'Tell me how it works at the moment', and 'What criteria should we apply in judging our ideas?'.

♦ **Closed questions.** These allow only a 'yes' or 'no' response from the person you are questioning. In general, try to avoid questions such as 'Do you think it is too difficult?', as they close down a discussion rather than open it up further.

♦ **Follow-up questions.** These allow you to probe further along a particular line of questioning. Perhaps when an open question does not get the group talking very much, you could be more specific with a follow-up question. Or you could use it to explore the 'yes' or 'no' response to a closed question. For instance, if someone comes up with an idea and you want them to elaborate, perhaps you could ask, 'Could you explain that in a bit more detail please?'. Other examples could include 'Why would we want to do that?', 'What would be the first step if we did choose to do it that way?', and 'Why do you think it would be difficult?'.

♦ **Hypothetical questions.** These are 'What if . . . ?', 'How would you feel if . . . ?' or 'What would you do if . . . ?' questions. These encourage participants to think about possibilities or opportunities that *might* arise in the future.

Beware of bad questions!

Not all questions are created equally. In particular, it is possible to ask **leading questions**. Take as an example the following: 'don't you agree that it would be too costly to continue with this plan of action?' Obviously, it is a statement that is masquerading as a question.

Such *leading questions give an illusion of a choice* in the matter, but they actually signal to the participants that you have a particular view that they should not be disagreeing with. In particular, if you are the team's manager, they may be thinking, 'Why should I stick my neck out to disagree with my boss?'.

Why? Why? Why? Why? Why?

The question 'why?' is one of the most powerful tools you can use to get to the bottom of what people are saying.

Taken to an extreme, some facilitators advocate using the **five whys** technique. It simply involves asking the question 'why?' up to five times to understand what a participant really means. Once you have understood the root cause of what the participant thinks, you can start to address what to do about it – perhaps by asking 'how could we . . . ?' questions.

An example

Let's consider the following conversation between a facilitator (F) and a participant (P) who initially doesn't agree:

P: 'It won't work.'
F: '*Why* won't it work?'
P: 'Because no one wants to do it!'
F: '*Why* do you think no one wants to do it?'
P: 'Because we don't have the time to do it.'

F: 'And *why* do you feel that people don't have the time?'

P: 'Because our suppliers never deliver the goods on time so we are always in a rush.'

F: 'Ah, okay. So how could we make it work then?'

P: 'Well, the only way I could see it working is if we could switch suppliers or change the contract we have with our current suppliers.'

That was actually only three 'whys' and one 'how'. So I'm not saying that you should necessarily ask five 'why?' questions in a row. Hopefully, though, the example does illustrate how important it is to question participants' statements rather than accepting them at face value. But do be careful that you do not come across too aggressively in your questioning. This is not an interrogation!

What you don't say is as important as what you do say

You need to listen carefully to ensure that you can follow the gist of the conversation. But, at the same time, you need to be using both **verbal and non-verbal techniques** to encourage every single participant within the group to talk openly.

Verbal techniques

By listening to what is being said and making appropriate comments, you can both encourage people and probe further. Try to:

♦ **Paraphrase.** This is a technique for checking that you have got the right end of the stick. You might, for instance, begin your sentence with something like 'So would it be correct to say that . . . ?' or 'It sounds like . . .'.

♦ **Link.** This involves taking something that someone said earlier in the discussion and referring back to it. For example, 'John said earlier that he wasn't very comfortable with the sales plan. Does anyone else feel the same way?'

♦ **Reward and reinforce.** When participants do come up with comments or ideas, you might want to say, 'thank you' or 'that's a good point', or offer them a smile or a nod to encourage them to continue with further contributions.

Non-verbal techniques

♦ **Use silence.** When you first ask a question, you might get faced with a period of silence, which could make you nervous that the group did not understand the question. You may be panicking and feel the need to fill the silence with another question or an example of what you mean. But remember that the group may need some time to mull the issue over and think of an appropriate answer. A period of silence feels much longer for the facilitator stood at the front of a group than it does for the group itself!

♦ **Avoid showing your disagreement.** Sometimes a participant may make a suggestion that is quite frankly dumb. But if you react by showing anger or irritation, you will only make the participants worry that they are being judged. The result will be that it stifles further discussion. So be careful not to show any negative emotions.

♦ **Look attentive.** Ensure that you look at the participant who is talking, and perhaps turn your body to face them. Failing to make eye contact or having an inappropriate posture can sometimes give the impression that you are bored or not listening.

Facilitation is definitely about asking, not telling

Sometimes you may know a lot about the topic of discussion. For example, you may be facilitating a group of colleagues in your own department or you may even be the company's expert in the area. So it is natural for you to want to contribute to the content, but facilitation is definitely not the same as lecturing people or telling them what you think.

As the facilitator, remember that *you are there to design and guide a process to allow other people to come up with the content*.

Why?

Often, a big problem is that people do not feel that they 'own' or 'buy into' ideas and actions. But, by allowing the participants to come up with their own ideas, they will feel more involved – more 'empowered' – and therefore more committed to turning those ideas into reality. In short, *you want their commitment, not their compliance.*

Think about it. Which would you prefer – to follow a course of action that you had decided upon yourself or one that someone else was instructing you to comply with?

Questioning to disagree

When you do have 'expert' knowledge, you can use it to guide a group without contributing directly to the content of the discussion. For example, if one of the participants has a strong point of view that you disagree with, you could throw a good question to the other participants in the group to see if they agree or not.

Here are a few examples of ways to steer a group using questions rather than stating your own opinions:

Bad contribution	Good question
'This is how we should do it.'	'How do you think we should do it?'
'I don't think that will work.'	'Can anyone else in the group see any difficulties with that suggestion?'
'We should start by . . .'	'How should we start?'
'What you've just said is wrong.'	'I get the sense that it may not be as easy as you say. Does anyone have any concerns about that?'

An example

If the idea of using expert questions rather than outright statements to disagree still doesn't make sense, let's consider the following example. It's an exchange between a participant (P) and a facilitator (F) who clearly does not agree.

P: 'Yes, we should go ahead and launch the new product.'

F: 'That's a very bold statement. Let's check if anyone else in the group has any concerns about that.'

At this stage, no one else in the group speaks up. But the facilitator has 'expert' knowledge on the topic and believes that money is a problem in funding the launch of the product. So the facilitator continues with a different question.

F: 'Okay, can I ask the group how we might finance it?'

P: 'Oh, we'll find the money somehow.'

F: 'But does everyone agree with that? Can I just ask some of the other people in the group? Michael? Simone? How comfortable do you feel about our ability to pay for the product launch?'

As you can see, the facilitator could continue to ask open-ended questions to direct the group's thinking until the vocal participant changes his or her mind. Or one of the other participants in the group might say something.

Choosing to contribute to the discussion

However, if the entire group really does seem to be in agreement, then you have two options to consider:

1 You could use a statement to explain your concerns. Perhaps introduce your concerns tactfully, for example, 'I'm just wondering whether we actually have the money to pay for the launch given that we're already over budget and the finance director has said no to other projects of a similar value.' Then ask the participants for their response – 'What do you think?'.

Or:

2 You may actually be wrong. Even though you have 'expert' knowledge in the particular area, you may need to consider that the group might be right.

Facilitation is not just about asking questions

There are times when the people in your workshop or focus group may need a bit of stronger guidance than just insightful questions. By observing the participants' interactions with each other, you may come to the realisation that you need to move the discussion along or encourage the group in a different direction.

However, it is one of the most difficult challenges for you as the facilitator – knowing when to let a discussion run its own course and when to alter its direction.

The following are some examples of when you might want to move things along:

♦ When you think the discussion is going nowhere. You might intervene by saying, 'I get the sense that we're talking in circles here. Is there any way that we can come to some interim agreement on this issue?'

♦ When time is running out. 'I'm just conscious that we were planning to finish by five o'clock today and that you all need to get away. It's already past three o'clock. Can I suggest that we move on to the next issue to make sure that we don't run out of time?'

♦ When you have expert knowledge and feel that the group is not responding to your clever questions. For example, if you disagree with something, you could say 'I don't know if this is appropriate, but my impression was that it just doesn't work that way because . . .'

Be confident enough in yourself to make comment when you don't think that your insightful questions on their own are enough.

In summary . . .

♦ Use open questions to get the discussion going.

♦ Using other questions to probe and investigate will encourage the group to explore their thinking further.

♦ In particular, asking a group 'why?' will help you to get at the root cause of the group's thinking.

♦ Telling a group what you want them to do will get their compliance; asking a group what they want to do will gain you their commitment.

♦ If you do add to the content of the discussion directly, keep in mind that you could be wrong.

♦ Ensure that both your words and body language encourage people to participate in the discussion.

♦ Observe the group dynamics to ensure that the discussion is not spiralling onto irrelevant topics.

♦ Do speak up when your questions are not enough on their own.

Chapter 4

Kicking Off on the Right Foot

In this chapter:

♦ **introducing a workshop**
♦ **setting objectives and getting buy-in**
♦ **setting people's expectations**
♦ **creating the right climate for discussion**
♦ **how ground rules can save the day**
♦ **breaking the ice**
♦ **getting a group on your side**

You have probably heard that, in job interviews, most interviewers make up their minds about a candidate in the first few minutes. The same could easily apply to a workshop if you're not careful – participants can form a bad impression of you based on how well the first half-hour or so of your workshop goes.

This chapter shows you how to get your workshop off to a flying start.

The first ten minutes are critical – so don't mess them up

Because *first impressions count*, it really does pay for you to know exactly what you are going to say in your introduction. If it is an important workshop or meeting, it is almost certainly worth jotting down a few notes to remind yourself of what you need to cover on the day.

General points to introduce

The sorts of areas that you need to cover are likely to include:

♦ **Background.** The participants may have questions about why they are there or what the purpose of the day is. If a project sponsor was involved in setting up the meeting, you may want to explain about their role too.
♦ **Timings of the workshop.** Even if you do not hand the group a copy of the agenda for the meeting, you may want to give them an idea of when breaks and/or lunch might be.
♦ **Topics for the workshop.** You will need to talk briefly about the process – any exercises or activities – that you are going to use. For example, you might want to give people some advance warning that there will be some brainstorming up until the morning coffee break, then discussion about a plan of action until lunchtime, finishing up with a discussion of roles and responsibilities before ending the meeting at three o'clock.

♦ **'Housekeeping' items.** If you are off-site, it is
   worth mentioning anything about an unfamiliar
   physical environment. For example, you might
   want to point out where in the building they
   can smoke or find the nearest toilets or fax
   machine.

Just think about it for a moment. If you had been
invited to a workshop, what would *you* like to know
at the start?

Explaining your role

You also need to explain your role as the facilitator –
especially if the people in your group are not familiar
with the concept of having a facilitator. If you
intend to act as a pure facilitator (i.e. not add any
content into the discussion), then you need to
explain not only that you are doing it but also the
reasons why.

If you are well acquainted with the participants in the
workshop – for example you are their manager or a
close colleague – you will have to be ready to fend off
their questions on content. They may ask for your
input on the content of the discussion – 'What do you
think?' But if you really do want to focus solely on the
process and group dynamics, you will have to remind
the group that you would rather not add to the
content of the discussion.

On the other hand, if you want to add your own
thoughts and ideas, you will need to mention this, as

many people expect facilitators to only facilitate and not actually take part in the discussion.

Using multimedia

The clever use of multimedia can spice up a workshop. For example:

♦ Showing the group a two-minute clip of an advert or television programme can often pique a group's interest.
♦ Presenting colour slides definitely looks more professional than hand-written overhead transparencies.

However, make sure that you are familiar with the workings of the audiovisual equipment, and turn up 30 minutes before the start of the workshop to check that it actually works. Don't rely on your audiovisual department or the conference organisers – because the participants will blame *you* if it all goes wrong. There is nothing so frustrating for a participant as watching a facilitator trying to figure out why some piece of equipment won't work.

Clear objectives will keep your workshop on track

You should, in most workshops, already have a good idea of the objectives. Perhaps you have agreed the objectives with the sponsor of the workshop. Or maybe you have done some research with the participants themselves.

In your introductions you certainly need to present these objectives. What is critical here is to *ensure that the participants all understand the objectives*. It is not good enough just to present them – as different participants may read and interpret them in slightly different ways. So it is a good idea to get the participants' initial thoughts on the objectives to ensure that they have a common understanding about the objectives.

You could check that participants really do understand the objectives by using a few questions:

♦ 'What do you think this objective actually means in practical terms?'
♦ 'Given these objectives, can anyone give me an example of the sorts of actions that we should be coming up with?'

Example objectives

A set of objectives for a training workshop might read as follows:

♦ To identify your current strengths and weaknesses in terms of interacting with customers.
♦ To develop your ability to build relationships with customers.
♦ To identify actions that you can take after the workshop to enhance your relationship building skills.

As another example, take a look at the objectives for a planning session:

- To brainstorm innovative ideas for raising our market share.
- To identify the top three options for boosting our market share.
- To sketch out a rough plan of action – including roles and responsibilities, budgets and timescales – for our favoured option.

Getting 'buy-in'

If the objectives have not been set in stone, you should ask the group for any amendments or additions to the objectives. Again, this will help to get their 'buy-in' to the workshop – getting their consent and commitment rather than mere compliance with the aims of the workshop. Ask questions such as:

- 'Is anything missing from this list of objectives?'
- 'Are these objectives reasonable for today's meeting?'
- 'Does anyone disagree with any of these objectives? Why? And how should it read instead?'

Expectations need to be set in both directions

Participants can sometimes have unreasonably high expectations of what they can get out of a workshop – they might, for instance, think that they should be able to solve just about everything that is wrong with their organisation. And it is not uncommon for them to blame the facilitator for not achieving those high expectations. So it is in your interest to discuss briefly what is *not* going to be covered in the workshop.

In particular, *you may want to talk about constraints or boundaries for the discussion*. Some examples:

♦ If the objective of the workshop is to identify ways to cut costs, your sponsor may have mentioned that moving the corporate HQ is *not* an option up for discussion.
♦ Perhaps the objective of a focus group is to think about how to implement a new corporate vision. But the chief executive may have said that the vision has already been agreed by the board and therefore cannot be changed.
♦ Or maybe the session is aimed at brainstorming ideas for improving customer service. But the IT director has said that a decision has already been taken to introduce a new telephone voicemail system by the end of the year.

In such cases, you need to highlight these 'no go' areas and warn the participants off from wasting too much time talking about them.

The group dynamics are critical for good discussion

We have already talked a little about the concept of group dynamics. The 'climate' within the workshop or meeting should enable all of the participants to speak openly and honestly in order to come up with ideas and solutions.

Unfortunately, the culture of an organisation often determines norms or unwritten rules of behaviour that can inhibit open discussion. For example, it is not uncommon for many employees to feel that:

♦ They should avoid contradicting the boss (because it is against your own best interests to make the boss unhappy).
♦ They should agree in order to avoid conflict (because conflict makes people unhappy and keen to get their own back).
♦ They should defer to more senior colleagues (because they have been around for longer and know better).

But these rules can stifle open discussion. So it is your job as the facilitator to *challenge any such inappropriate norms* and encourage frank discussion regardless of participants' seniority or job titles, or even a bit of disagreement.

Ground rules can formalise discussions about group dynamics

In running a particularly tricky workshop, it may be worth having a more formalised discussion about how the discussion should be governed. In such situations, many facilitators will try to get the participants to agree on **ground rules** or **principles as to what is acceptable or unacceptable behaviour** within the group.

Many people have heard of ground rules. Perhaps you could get the discussion going by asking:

♦ 'How many people have heard of ground rules? And how would you define ground rules?'
♦ 'What sorts of ground rules would be appropriate for this meeting?'
♦ 'How are we going to enforce the ground rules when people fail to live up to them?'

When the participants suggest and agree such rules, it is worth writing these up – perhaps on a flip chart sheet for all to see during the workshop. Then when someone breaches the rules, perhaps inadvertently, you should gently remind the offender about them.

If someone persistently offends, you may need to make more strident efforts to enforce them. If it gets really bad, you could ask the rest of the group what they want to do with the individual. Or you might even need to throw the individual out of the group, if his or her behaviour is affecting everyone else's ability to get on with the discussion.

Example ground rules

Some typical ground rules include:

♦ Talk openly regardless of seniority within the group.
♦ Anyone can disagree with anyone else – if they give a reason.
♦ Mobile phones off.
♦ No personal attacks on other participants. It is okay

to disagree with someone, but saying 'that's a ridiculous idea' or 'the problem with you is . . .' is just offensive.

♦ Speak honestly within the workshop without fear of reprisal afterwards.

♦ Respect time-keeping, eg coming back in 20 minutes if the group has agreed to only take a 20-minute break.

♦ The discussion 'goes no further than these four walls'. This may be particularly appropriate on sensitive issues.

Don't just be tempted to throw all of these up on to a sheet of flip chart paper though. Some of them may be entirely inappropriate for your group. For example, if one of the participants is waiting for an important call from a client, he or she might rather not be in the workshop than miss the call. Or if a senior person in the workshop is known for vengeful behaviour, then writing up 'speak honestly without fear of reprisal' is simply not going to convince the other participants that it really is okay to be as candid as they might otherwise like.

Use icebreakers to get things moving

Often the participants may not have met each other before, or have only a passing familiarity with each other. Or it may be that you have never met the participants in the group. In such cases it is worth investing a few minutes in an 'icebreaker' to get the participants acquainted and more comfortable talking to each other.

There are hundreds of ways to break the ice. Just ask some of your colleagues what icebreakers they have experienced. The type of icebreaker that you choose to use depends on several factors:

♦ How long is the workshop going to run for? If the entire workshop is only half a day long, you don't want to waste more than a few minutes on a quick icebreaker. But if the workshop is going to last three days, you can more comfortably spend half-an-hour on an icebreaker.
♦ How formal are the participants? How well (or badly) would a 'wacky' or 'zany' icebreaker go down with the participants? A group of graduates, for instance, might be happy to play a fun game, whereas a group of senior executives might only be comfortable with giving their name and a few words on their careers.

Example icebreakers

Some of the more popular icebreakers include:

♦ **Introducing yourself.** Perhaps ask each participant in turn to tell the group their name, their job title and a bit about their current role. You could vary it by asking people to talk about their experience with the topic of discussion. During a training session you might also want to get them to talk about their personal aims for the workshop.

♦ **Introducing your neighbour.** A common alternative is to ask participants to interview the person sitting next to them. Then ask the participant to introduce their neighbour, and vice versa.

♦ **Drawing pictures.** You could ask the participants to take part in a more light-hearted – yet effective – way of learning a bit more about each other. Give the participants a sheet of flip chart paper and then ask them to draw a picture that represents their work and home lives. Once they have drawn their pictures, get each person to talk to the group for a few minutes about what the pictures represent.

It really is up to you to choose what will suit your participants the best.

The icebreaker is particularly useful if you have difficulty remembering names. It is a good opportunity to take a few brief notes as the participants introduce themselves. You could even draw a sketch of the seating plan and scribble each participant's name on your diagram. But if you really have difficulty remembering names, you could encourage each participant to fill out a name placard where they are sitting or even issue each participant with a name badge.

Get the group on your side as quickly as you can

Sometimes you may be invited to facilitate a workshop with participants who you have never met before. If this is the case, you need to win them over as quickly as possible.

Doing research with the participants beforehand will help. But here are some more tips for getting the group on your side as quickly as possible:

1 **Introduce yourself as well as your role.** The group may be wondering 'why have *you* been asked to facilitate this group?' So you may want to explain briefly about your background and experience of facilitating other (successful) workshops or meetings.

2 **Encourage group responsibility from the start.** After saying something about what you can do as a facilitator, you can say to the group: 'I'm going to try to keep the discussion on track, but here's what I'd like you all to do to help make this workshop a success.' Then list how you would like them to contribute – such as speaking honestly and not harbouring doubts silently, etcetera. You could perhaps do this as part of gathering ground rules for the workshop.

3 **Use information about each participant as quickly as possible.** Use their first names whenever you can. Or, if you can remember anything about the participants, try to incorporate that information into your facilitation. For example,

'Steve, in your experience as a manager, do you have a different perspective on this?'

In summary . . .

♦ **Spend some time thinking about how you will introduce the background to the workshop and your role during it.**

♦ **Communicate objectives clearly and get the group to agree to them for a successful workshop.**

♦ **Make the participants aware of any constraints to the discussion.**

♦ **Ensure open and honest discussion for a productive workshop.**

♦ **Use ground rules to challenge inappropriate norms that might otherwise inhibit open discussion.**

♦ **Choose carefully an icebreaker that is appropriate for your particular group.**

♦ **If you do not already know the participants, get to know them as quickly as you can.**

Chapter 5

Livening Things Up with Tools and Techniques

In this chapter:

- **harnessing creativity through good old brainstorming**
- **attacking brainstorming from different angles**
- **using the SWOT**
- **choosing to use a PEST or PESTLE**
- **looking through the Diagnostic Window at what can change**
- **breaking down processes with brown papering**

Some groups can come up with new ideas when simply asked an open question such as 'What ideas do we have to . . . ?'. Others can talk for hours when asked 'How could we improve . . . ?'. But many groups find that they need a bit more structure. A good facilitator will use activities or exercises, incorporating tools and techniques into the process, in order to generate a greater quantity or quality of ideas and suggestions.

This is not to say that you must always use tools or techniques. Perhaps you might start a workshop off with a bit of open discussion around an issue, then delve into one tool to analyse an issue in more depth, before finishing off with another round of discussion. Or you might choose to use tool after tool after tool.

Whatever you choose, these tools are here for you to use, as you will.

Brainstorming is great for creative ideas

Brainstorming is one of the most popular techniques for encouraging creativity. The aim is to generate *as many ideas as possible* without worrying initially about the quality of each idea. Only when the group has finished coming up with new ideas should they spend time looking at how good each idea might be.

The reason for doing this is because – in many cases – the best idea for tackling a problem can sometimes be the most supposedly 'obvious' or 'silly' idea.

Although most people have heard of brainstorming, it is worth spending a few minutes explaining the rules to your participants:

1 **Every idea is recorded.** Every idea, no matter how 'bad', 'obvious', or 'stupid', should be written down.
2 **No idea is evaluated** during the brainstorming. Only when either you or the participants have agreed to stop coming up with new ideas should you go back over the list to evaluate them.

Brainstorming sessions should be just a little bit frantic. As the facilitator, you should be encouraging the participants to shout ideas out to you as quickly as you can write them down. And, if anyone does start to evaluate or judge the ideas, remind them – politely but firmly – not to.

Brainstorming comes in many different guises

The traditional form of brainstorming involves having participants shouting ideas out at the facilitator, but there are common variants of brainstorming.

One of the most popular in recent years involves the Post-It note. Each participant could be given a pad of Post-It notes along with a thick marker pen. The facilitator then encourages each individual to write ideas down for say five minutes, with each fresh idea on a separate Post-It.

Then the participants could stick them up on a wall or a white board to look at the mass of ideas. Using this variant, it is possible for even a small group to come up with literally hundreds of ideas in only a few minutes.

Clustering ideas

If participants are asked individually to generate ideas on Post-It notes, there could be a lot of overlap between the suggestions made by different people. You may therefore want to ask the group to look over the many Post-Its to find any identical suggestions and remove the duplicates.

Another useful technique is to ask the group to 'cluster' or gather related ideas together. Groups often find it easier to talk about a half-dozen groups of ideas rather than dozens and dozens of individual ideas.

SWOT diagram: a tool for analysing an organisation

The SWOT diagram gets its name because it involves analysing the **strengths, weaknesses, opportunities and threats** of an organisation, team or group of people. It is a particularly useful (and popular) tool for starting off a discussion of *what is right or wrong with an organisation*. Perhaps this could then lead into a debate about ways of making the organisation better or more successful.

Here is how to do a SWOT analysis:

1 Draw a two-by-two matrix on a flipchart and then write one of the labels into each of the four boxes as follows.

Strengths	Weaknesses
Opportunities	Threats

2 Explain that *strengths and weaknesses are attributes that are internal to the organisation; opportunities and threats are issues external to the organisation* that might affect it.

3 Ask the group to brainstorm aspects of the organisation that fit into each of the boxes.

Using the SWOT analysis

Sometimes participants may disagree about whether a particular aspect of the organisation fits into one box or another. For example, a participant might initially suggest that the chief executive is a strength of the organisation because of his dominant personality – but another participant might say that the chief executive's stubbornness should be listed as a weakness. In such cases it is okay to put it into both boxes.

As the facilitator you should avoid letting participants become too hung-up about exactly where a particular comment goes. Capture it first; debate its position on the grid later.

Varying the SWOT analysis

The SWOT analysis is commonly run from the viewpoint of the participants in the group. However, it is sometimes valuable to get a more rounded perspective by asking your group to think about the strengths, weaknesses, opportunities and threats from other points of view such as:

♦ The organisation's customers.

♦ The organisation's or team's competitors.
♦ The bosses (as opposed to the employees).

You can also apply the SWOT analysis to groups other than the organisation. For example, other groups could include:

♦ A department or division.
♦ A team.
♦ Or even an individual.

PEST diagram: understanding the external environment

PEST gets its name because it is an analysis of the **political, economic, social, and technological** factors that could affect the external environment around an organisation or group.

Political	Economic
Social	Technological

PESTLE

PESTLE is just a variation of the PEST diagram, adding to the discussion the **legal and environmental** factors that can affect the future of the organisation.

Political	Economic	Social
Technological	Legal	Environmental

While it can be useful to consider these additional elements, don't automatically choose to use the PESTLE instead of the PEST analysis. Ask yourself: do you *really* need to analyse legal and environmental factors? Or would talking about them merely waste time that could be better spent concentrating on the political, economic, social and technological factors?

Diagnostic Window: a matrix for understanding what can change

The Diagnostic Window is another two-by-two matrix for analysing what is good or bad about a situation. But by looking at both *aspects that can be changed as well as aspects that cannot be changed*, it helps to focus the group on the priorities for action.

	Aspects we can change	Aspects we can't change
Good aspects of the situation	1	2
Bad aspects of the situation	3	4

The four boxes, numbered 1 to 4, are filled out as follows.

Box 1

This represents good aspects of the situation that people want to change – i.e. improve. For example, if a group of company employees think that the pension scheme is good, but could be even better, then the comment would go into this box.

Box 2

This second box should be used to capture aspects of the situation that are good, but that either cannot or should not be tampered with. For example, the group of employees might argue that the canteen is good enough, and therefore not worth improving.

Box 3

This box is for aspects of the organisation that are unsatisfactory and need improvement. A typical list of items might include 'Poor communication between teams' or 'Lack of involvement in decision-making'.

Box 4

This final box is for bad aspects of the organisation that either cannot be changed or that participants feel are not worth investing too much effort into trying to alter. As an example, employees might say that there are 'insufficient parking spaces', but perhaps this is something governed by town planning rules rather than the organisation's policy.

If the Diagnostic Window is filled out correctly, a group wanting to make the situation better should naturally focus on the items within box number 3, followed by box number 1. Because the items in boxes 2 and 4 are essentially unchangeable or require too much effort to change, they can effectively be ignored or put on hold until the items in boxes 3 and 1 have been sorted out.

Brown papering helps you improve processes

Brown papering is a technique for describing the individual steps within a process so that you can then improve it. It provides *a visual depiction of the steps* required to make a process happen.

For example, a process could be about how packages are dispatched from a warehouse when customers telephone to place orders. Or it could be about how candidates are handed over from the HR department to line managers for interviewing. By laying out all of the steps, a group can *identify bottlenecks or areas of inefficiency* and then make changes to the overall process, perhaps to save time or money.

This technique originally got its name from the long sheets of brown paper (often many metres!) that people used to put up on walls to write on. Thankfully, the advent of the Post-It note means that we can dispense with the brown paper. But the name has remained.

Running a brown papering session

Facilitating a session of brown papering might go as follows:

1 Get the group thinking about an overall process that needs to be made more effective – perhaps quicker or cheaper. The process could be as simple as how letters are moved from the post room into employees' in-trays around the office.
2 Then get the group to brainstorm the steps involved onto individual Post-It notes. For example, these might include 'empty post bag into sorting office' and 'take letters up to each floor in lift'.
3 Ask the participants to put the Post-Its up on a wall or white board, from left to right, in the order in which they need to occur to make the overall process happen.
4 Once you have identified all of the individual steps, you can look at ways of reducing the number of steps. Perhaps write in new Post-It notes and replace overly complicated ways of doing things.

As the facilitator, you should think of good questions to ask to make sure that the group does not leave out any steps along the way.

In summary . . .

♦ Use tools and techniques to provide some structure to a group's thinking.

♦ Brainstorming is great for generating lots of ideas.

♦ Post-It notes are a valuable addition to brainstorming sessions – making the best of both group and individual creativity.

♦ The SWOT matrix is a good starting point for comprehensively understanding an organisation or group.

♦ Apply PEST and PESTLE analyses to understand the environment around an organisation.

♦ Use the Diagnostic Window to focus a group's attention on what most needs changing.

♦ Run a brown papering session when you need to improve the speed or cost-effectiveness of a process.

Chapter 6

Injecting Energy into Meetings and Workshops

In this chapter:

♦ **mixing the groups up**

♦ **getting people up on their feet**

♦ **using role playing to good effect**

♦ **changing gears**

♦ **building breaks into your process**

♦ **creating your own tools and techniques**

Tools and techniques are the building blocks of a workshop process. But simply learning and applying such tools and techniques is not enough to get good results from the content of the discussion. Outstanding facilitation is about manipulating both process *and* group dynamics.

Participants get bored and tired very quickly. Imagine how you would feel if you were asked to sit around a table for eight hours with only an hour for lunch and a couple of quick coffee breaks?

As part of managing group dynamics, you need to design your process to *incorporate different twists on traditional tools and techniques to keep people interested.*

Introducing these variations should have a dramatic effect on the productivity of your participants.

Splitting your group up will add variety

Rather than having one big discussion, you could split the participants into different sub-groups to allow smaller discussions to run in parallel. The sub-groups do not necessarily have to leave the main room – they could just move to different corners of the same room, for instance.

Syndicate group work

Splitting the main group into two smaller 'syndicate' (also called 'breakout') groups has two main benefits:

♦ It allows people to have more 'air time' – because there are fewer people in each smaller group trying to speak at once.
♦ And it allows each syndicate group to tackle different issues in parallel, using the time allotted for the workshop more effectively.

You could divide the main group up to cover an issue each. After a period of discussion, you could ask each syndicate group to write up the highlights of their discussion on a sheet of flip chart paper. Then they could nominate someone to present the results of their discussion back to the main group. But then, most critically, as the facilitator you should get a discussion going in the main group to *ensure that differences of opinion or comments from the other group are aired.*

Pair work

Working in pairs is just an extension of syndicate group work. Rather than dividing the main group into two syndicates, you can divide them into pairs. This is particularly useful when the group has a lot of ground to cover and time is short.

Each pair could discuss a different issue, problem or part of a topic. For example, if you had eight people in your group and needed to do a SWOT analysis, you could ask the group to split into four pairs to work on one segment of the SWOT diagram each.

After a pair discussion, it is always a good idea for you to facilitate a brief round-up of what suggestions each pair came up with.

Get them up on their feet to keep them from falling asleep

People simply get tired of sitting at a table for long periods of time. One easy way to keep a group engaged with a discussion is to incorporate physical movement into your workshop.

In particular, techniques that require a group to get up on their feet are particularly useful during the so-called **graveyard slot** – the hour or so just after lunch. Participants very often feel sleepy after having filled their stomachs, so productivity may not be at its highest.

Two popular methods for getting groups moving are:

1 Roving brainstorm

This is a useful technique for getting every participant involved. You begin by writing up a number of issues on separate flip chart sheets, then putting them up on the walls. For example, in a teambuilding workshop you might have separate sheets for 'behaviours that promote teamworking', 'behaviours that hinder teamworking' and 'how we could change the office environment to enhance teamworking'.

Then give each participant a marker pen and ask them to move around the room, writing their suggestions or comments on the sheets of paper. Allow the participants a period of time – for example fifteen minutes or so for straightforward issues to perhaps half-an-hour for more complex issues – to rove around the room, marking their comments up.

Then you could summon the group together again to discuss the responses on each sheet of paper. As the facilitator, your job is then to use these comments to promote further discussion.

2 Market stalls

This is a variant of the roving brainstorm. Again, separate issues are written up on separate flip chart sheets and put up on the walls of the room. But rather than allowing every participant to work on every flip chart, you divide the group up into a number of syndicates to work on an issue each.

After each syndicate has had enough time to start tackling the issue on their flip chart sheet, you ask one member of the syndicate to stay with the flip chart sheet, but ask the other members of the syndicate to move to a new flip chart sheet. In this way one participant stays to look after or 'tend' the market stall, while the other participants move to a different market stall to discuss the comments that have been written up by the initial syndicate and perhaps amend or add to those initial comments.

Your role during a market stalls session is to ensure that participants know whether they are supposed to be staying to tend their stall or moving to comment on other stalls.

Use role playing with caution

A lot of people are quite cynical about role playing, so be warned that not everyone responds well to it! Having said that though, you can skilfully employ a bit of role playing to good effect to get people thinking in different ways.

Certain workshops are particularly suited to role playing:

♦ During a **training or development workshop** aimed at teaching participants new skills. You can use role playing to help participants practise a new skill – for example, coaching or disciplining team members. It will help your participants if

beforehand you have prepared some notes on the
scenario that they are supposed to be role-playing.

♦ When you want to make the participants
understand a **different point of view**. For
example, when your group is trying to come up
with a new product, you may want them to
understand how a customer or consumer might
respond to it. So why not get them to role-play
briefly what their initial response to the new
product might be?

Participants sometimes report that they feel foolish
doing role play. So you must *explain why you are asking
them to do the role play and how it fits into the context of
your overall workshop*. And then remind them of the
purpose after they have completed the role play too.

You need to slow things down as well as speed things up

Activities such as dividing your group into syndicates
or the roving brainstorm work well when you need to
increase the pace of the workshop. But there are times
when you may also want to slow the pace down.

It can be important to let people think about the
implications of a complex issue rather than wade into a
debate with only half-baked ideas. You might also
want to slow down when the discussion is getting too
raucous or perhaps the participants are losing focus.

Some ideas for slowing down a workshop:

♦ Give the participants information on handouts to read and reflect upon. Examples could include perhaps a relevant newspaper clipping or just a copy of your company's vision statement.

♦ Ask the participants to brainstorm on their own. Ask them to write their ideas on single Post-It notes for a few minutes before collating them for discussion.

♦ Show the participants a short video clip, but make sure that it lasts no more than four or five minutes – or your participants may end up falling asleep.

♦ Hand out a questionnaire with boxes to tick and score. Typically, questionnaires provide people with rating scales, for example '1 = agree, 2 = neither agree nor disagree, 3 = disagree' or perhaps simple 'yes or no'.

♦ Invent a short quiz that requires each participant to write down answers to a series of open questions, for example 'What do you think are the three major barriers to increasing productivity?' or 'Who are the key stakeholders in making this new service a success?'.

Break things up to keep things going

Your participants are only human. If you ask them to work for more than a couple of hours in a row, no matter how many different techniques you use to keep people engaged, fatigue will strike. And don't forget that people need toilet breaks every couple of hours or so. So you must plan breaks into your workshops.

Use your initiative to introduce spontaneous, unplanned breaks when you feel that the participants need one. If, for example, you sense that energy levels are low – perhaps after a particularly difficult discussion – it might make sense to convene a quick ten-minute coffee break. Or, if a group is being particularly tired and unproductive, perhaps ask them whether it would make more sense to finish the meeting for the day and perhaps pick up another time.

But do not follow your planned breaks slavishly. Sometimes a group may be in the middle of a particularly productive discussion and willing to work through a break.

Allowing ideas to incubate

If you have a lot of material to cover in your process, it is often a good idea to space it out over a number of weeks or months rather than rushing through it all at once.

You may want to introduce gaps between separate workshop sessions because:

♦ You want to give the participants an opportunity to try out new skills. For example, if you are running a training workshop on presentation skills, you might run the first day of a workshop then ask them to try out their newly honed presentation skills. After several weeks you might come back for a second workshop session to review progress and refine those skills further.

♦ On a tough decision, the participants may need time out to let the ideas 'incubate'. They may want time to reflect before taking a difficult decision.

♦ Or you might need the participants to take action outside of the workshop or meeting before the discussion can move on. Perhaps in your first meeting you have established that there are three options to investigate. You, for example, then want to give the participants a month to gather information and analyse data on which is the best option before a final meeting to discuss which one to plan out in detail.

So think about whether your process should consist of, for example, one three-day workshop, or three one-day workshops or even six half-day workshops.

Tools and techniques are endlessly flexible

We have covered a few tools and techniques and Chapters 9 and 12 present a few more, but you shouldn't feel that you have to follow them to the letter. *These tools and techniques are not written in stone.* So if you don't think that a particular tool is quite right for your group, change it – do it *your* way.

For example, if you just need to understand the external factors affecting your company, why not just look at opportunities and threats rather than do a full

SWOT analysis? No one has said that the 'E' in the PEST diagram has got to be about economic factors – why not *ecological* factors if you think it's relevant?

Adapt these tools to your own purposes. Does a particular tool or technique suit the temperament of your group? Or can you add a twist to it to make it more applicable or perhaps more convenient for the group's needs?

Variables you could mix up

Why not combine tools and techniques to keep your group interested in the work at hand? As just a couple of examples, you could:

♦ Split a main group into four syndicates to do a SWOT analysis, so one group covers only strengths, another group looks at weaknesses, etc. After 20 minutes you could ask people to swap groups.
♦ Add a completely new spin to a tool or technique, perhaps by getting people to draw pictures that represent their ideas rather than just talking about them.
♦ Invite volunteers to facilitate parts of the overall workshop – say for half-an-hour or so. This will almost certainly get them more engaged with the discussion and force them to pay attention.
♦ Give them a video camera to record and play back any syndicate presentation that they may be putting together.

Considering the experience and open-mindedness of your participants, what else might work for *you* and *your group?*

In summary . . .

♦ **Invite syndicate groups or pairs to discuss issues in parallel to cover more ground.**

♦ **Introduce physical movement into your workshop or meeting to jolt the group awake.**

♦ **Role playing can be used in certain circumstances to help a group learn or discuss more effectively.**

♦ **Use techniques to both slow down as well as speed up the pace of a workshop.**

♦ **Allow breaks so that empty stomachs, full bladders and sleepy brains don't get in the way of the topic of discussion.**

♦ **Variations on tools and techniques are only limited by your imagination.**

♦ **But do ask yourself whether any variation will be appropriate to the culture of the participants.**

Chapter 7

Dealing with Difficult People

In this chapter:

- ◆ **observing group dynamics**
- ◆ **digging for workshop dirt**
- ◆ **managing loud or aggressive people**
- ◆ **getting the best out of quiet people**
- ◆ **recognising your impact on others**

Remember in Chapter 1 we talked about content, process and group dynamics – the three critical elements for successful facilitation? Because if you don't pay attention to how the participants are feeling and interacting with each other, you could risk losing their concentration or enthusiasm. And, in turn, the output of the group will fall.

Is every single participant giving the discussion their full attention and making an equal contribution? If there is even one participant pushing their own personal agenda too much, there are bound to be losers in the discussion – other participants having to take a back seat to it all.

By being aware of how the group *should* be behaving and is *actually* behaving, you can help the group to be as productive as it can be.

Keep an eye out for how people are feeling

What are the participants saying and how are they saying it? Listen to the words that the participants use, as well as their tone of voice. Do they sound at all bored or aggressive, fed-up or worried?

Look out for overt signs that participants are becoming agitated – about either the content of the discussion or the process you have developed to guide the discussion. Be on guard for phrases such as:

◆ 'I don't think we're covering the right topics.'
◆ 'We're not spending enough time talking about . . .'
◆ 'We're wasting time discussing this. What we should be doing is talking about how to . . .'

Watch non-verbal behaviours too

In addition to what they actually say, look out for the following 'non-verbal' aspects of how the group is behaving:

◆ Is anyone yawning, fidgeting or continually glancing at the clock or their watch? Look out for the classic signs of boredom and perhaps think about increasing the pace of the meeting.
◆ Are any of the participants engaging in side-conversations or private jokes? If they are, they

are probably not fully engaged in the process of your workshop or meeting.

♦ Have any of the participants ceased making contributions to the discussion? Sometimes, when participants disagree with the content of the discussion, they may decide to sit back and stop talking – effectively thinking, 'I can't be bothered with this'.

When you spot any signs that the group dynamic is becoming unhealthy, try to make some changes to your process to improve it so that the discussion can get on track again.

Use breaks to unearth issues

The most powerful method for understanding how your participants are feeling is to ask them. Breaks or lunches, or even drinks at the bar and dinners if you are running a lengthy workshop, are valuable opportunities to do so.

Perhaps take one person aside for a few minutes. Or talk to a sub-group of just a few people on an informal basis. Think about asking them questions such as:

♦ 'How are you finding the workshop so far?'
♦ 'Do you think we're covering the right sorts of issues?'
♦ 'How does this workshop compare with others that you have attended?'

♦ 'Is there anything that I could be doing better to help everyone get more out of the workshop?'

Again, once you have gathered some 'intelligence' on how they are feeling, try to make changes. Either:

♦ Make some changes to the rest of your workshop process to respond to any concerns they may have. For example, you might increase the pace or slow it down. Or use different techniques to what you had planned.
♦ Alternatively, deal with the individual by changing your style of facilitation during the workshop. The rest of this chapter focuses on tips for dealing with particular types of difficult people.

Loud participants can often be straightforward to handle

Participants who talk too much can derail a workshop. They can spend so much time talking that no one else has the chance to voice their opinions. If you don't deal effectively with these participants, the group could end up making a decision that only the minority actually agrees with.

So think about how to deal effectively with some of the different types of overly dominant participants:

1 The aggressive type
This person may be behaving aggressively towards either you or the other participants. It might be just a

few too many rude or disparaging remarks about you or the process; or perhaps it is frequent put-downs aimed at the other participants.

A participant who is being hostile towards you may resent the fact that an external person has been brought in to deal with an issue that he or she thinks should have been dealt with internally. Or perhaps they have just always got away with bullying other people.

When faced with this type of person, try to:

♦ Tackle the aggressive behaviour as soon as you can. If you have established ground rules about acceptable and non-acceptable behaviour, politely remind the aggressive participant that his or her behaviour is not in keeping with them.
♦ Ask the aggressive participant directly what the problem is. There may be a good reason for their aggression – perhaps they are frustrated with the pace of the workshop. Phrase a careful question along the lines of, 'I get the sense that you're not happy with the progress of the workshop. Is there something that we as a group could be doing differently?'
♦ Modify your process to reduce their impact on the other participants. For example, split the participants into a number of syndicate groups, and separate the aggressive participant from any of the more timid ones.

2 The so-called expert

Some participants just think that they know it all. In their eyes the whole workshop may be a waste of time as they think that they personally have all of the answers.

If you come across participants who think they know it all, you should:

♦ Respect the participant's need to be recognised as an expert. Thank the participant for their contribution, then try to get other participants involved. For example, you might say, 'Thank you for that, Judy. Can I ask what other people apart from Judy think about that?'.

♦ Avoid eye contact. Having eye contact is a powerful non-verbal cue giving permission to talk. Conversely, avoiding eye contact takes away that permission to talk.

♦ Try not to disagree with the person directly. Instead, use the other participants in the group to do the disagreeing. Perhaps say something like, 'That's an interesting point of view, what do other people think?'.

♦ Give the 'expert' a role in your meeting – such as taking minutes for you or operating any audio-visual equipment. This could distract them from talking too much.

3 The cynic

The cynic may claim to have seen other, similar initiatives fail in the past. They may be thinking that the entire workshop is a waste of time because the team or organisation will never actually succeed in changing or doing anything.

Some tips for handling cynics who think they have seen it all before:

♦ Don't let the cynic get away with criticising without justifying his or her reasons for feeling that way. If, for example, the cynic says, 'It will never work', you should ask, 'Why do you say that, Simon?'.

♦ Acknowledge the cynic's comments, and get the rest of the group involved in dealing with the problem. 'That's certainly a concern that Krishnan has raised. Does anyone else have any ideas on how we could tackle that?'.

♦ Modify your process to reduce the cynic's influence over others. Asking the group to brainstorm ideas on to Post-It notes is a good way to give the other participants an opportunity to express their opinions.

♦ Try to encourage the entire group to focus on the positive rather than the negative, perhaps by saying, 'It's easy to get bogged down in the problems and what won't work, but it's important that we focus on the positive. So how could we make this work?'.

Participants can be quiet for all sorts of reasons

A person who is not saying much could be agreeing with everything that is being said. Perhaps they think that the workshop is going so well that they don't need to speak. On the other hand, they may be fuming at how badly they think you are facilitating the workshop. Or perhaps they are just shy and worried about being shown up.

With participants who are very quiet, it is therefore critical that you try to uncover the reason for their silence before you can take action. Do they fit into any of the following categories?

1 The shy/inexperienced type

Some participants feel that they don't have much to contribute to a discussion because they are new to the organisation or more junior than the other participants in the group. Or perhaps they are just naturally shy.

Some ideas for helping to bring out a shy or inexperienced participant:

♦ Praise the quiet participant when he or she does make any contributions – 'That's a good point, David.'
♦ Occasionally ask them if they agree with what is being said. 'Xavier, the rest of the group seem to be doing a lot of the talking. Are you happy with the decision?' Hopefully they should at least be able to

say 'yes' or 'no' without too much embarrassment. Say their name before you ask the question (rather than asking the question then attaching their name to the end of the question), to give them more time to think.

♦ Make sure that your body language encourages them to speak. Make eye contact and perhaps give them a smile. And keep your tone of voice friendly towards them at all times.

♦ Modify your process to get their opinions without asking them to compete with the other participants for an opportunity to speak. Ask the group to brainstorm their ideas individually onto Post-It notes. Or divide the group up into pairs, and make the quiet participant work with someone friendly and supportive.

2 The lazy type

This participant just cannot be bothered. It could be because they do not feel any personal sense of responsibility. Or maybe they always try to get away with as little effort as possible in everything that they do.

Tips for dealing with a lazy participant:

♦ Give them tasks to do during the workshop. For example, if you are asking syndicate groups or pairs to report back, you could select the participants to report back, rather than ask for volunteers to do it.

♦ Direct questions at any lazy participants to keep them on their feet. 'We've heard from most of the people in the room on the subject. But Steve, what do you think?'

♦ Assign them a role that forces them to keep up with the discussion – such as taking minutes or notes for the workshop.

3 The silent rebel

This participant is the worst of all. He or she may be secretly disagreeing with everything that you are saying, but they may have decided that the whole workshop process is so pointless that it is not even worth their effort to pretend to be interested. The problem comes after the workshop – they are sure to be complaining about you and your process behind your back, undermining the good work of the other participants.

If you do identify a silent rebel, try to:

♦ Target them with specific questions, using their name to force them to voice any frustrations – for example, 'Nicola, I notice that you haven't said whether you agree or disagree with the decision. What do you think about it?'

♦ Ask the participant what the problem is. They usually feel that they have a good reason for their silence. You could ask them a careful question such as, 'I really want to make this workshop a success for everyone and I get the feeling that you aren't getting very much out of it. How could we make this workshop better for you?'

Be careful that *you* aren't the difficult person!

When the participants in a group do not seem to be responding very well in your workshop, it may be your process that needs to change. You could think about introducing (or taking out) some tools or techniques, and perhaps changing the pace too.

There are though occasions when the participants may have a problem with *you and your style of facilitation*.

It may be worth trying to answer for yourself some of the following questions:

♦ In your efforts to keep the workshop moving, are you trying to hurry the group too much? In your haste are you talking over participants, cutting them off, or finishing their sentences off for them?
♦ Are you using humour that is at all inappropriate for the workshop?
♦ Are you trying to enforce a process that is no longer appropriate for the group? If the discussion is moving in a different (but useful) direction to what you had expected and planned for, are you allowing it and supporting the group in their change of direction?
♦ Are you praising only some of the participants for their contributions and not others?
♦ Are you paying too much attention to the logic and content of the discussion? Are you observing and responding sufficiently to the group dynamics?

If you are answering 'yes' to any of these questions, then change your behaviour immediately.

In summary . . .

♦ Group dynamics is as important as the process for allowing the right content to emerge from the discussion.

♦ Watch each participant's behaviour during the workshop – is everyone contributing equally?

♦ Use breaks to find out how participants are feeling about your facilitation of the workshop.

♦ To handle a loud or disruptive participant, encourage the other participants to get more involved in the discussion.

♦ Try to find out why a participant is not contributing much to a discussion before you deal with them.

♦ Watch out that your personal style of facilitation is not having a negative impact on the group.

Chapter 8

Handling Sticky Situations

In this chapter:

♦ **resolving conflict between members of your group**

♦ **how can I use 'off-line' discussions to best effect?**

♦ **when is it okay to throw someone out of the group?**

♦ **handling challenges to your authority**

♦ **dealing with external pressures**

Outright conflict is probably the situation that facilitators fear the most. An element of debate and disagreement is essential for a good discussion – a little *divergence of opinion challenges bad ideas and entrenched ways of thinking*. But when it starts to get personal you will need to step in to prevent the conflict from spiralling out of control.

A different sort of conflict – conflict of interest – can also occur when pressures outside of the workshop impinge on the ability of the participants to have a productive discussion. When this happens, you may need to take more drastic action to salvage what you can of the workshop.

Deal with conflict quickly and quietly

When participants get into a shouting match and refuse to back down, it is up to you, as the facilitator, to step in and make sure that the conflict does not disrupt the entire workshop.

Don't intervene too quickly as the situation might (hopefully) resolve itself. However, if it continues to get worse:

♦ Look out for emotional language and stamp it out. If, for example, the participants resort to any name-calling, swearing or derogatory comments, you might interject with, 'I'm sorry, but that sort of language is not constructive. Could we focus on the topic without personal attacks please?' If possible, also get the offending party to apologise.

♦ Interrupt the argument to refer back to the objectives of the meeting if the conflict is taking the discussion off-course.

♦ Encourage one person to talk at a time. 'I'm sorry to interrupt, but I don't think that having the two of you talk at once is productive. Perhaps I could ask David to state his opinion first. And then I'll ask Natasha to respond. Could I ask you both to bear with me please?'

♦ Try to get other members of the group involved in the discussion. 'We seem to have reached a bit of a deadlock here, with David and Natasha presenting strongly opposite views. Can anyone else see a way out of this?'

What else could *you* do to manage conflict when it occurs during your workshops?

Use 'off-line' discussions to target difficult people

When participants are being difficult there is only so much that you can do during a workshop, with all of the other participants looking on. After all, an important principle in working with other people is to *praise publicly, but criticise privately*. So you might want to call a break – Americans would call it a 'time out' – and then have an 'off-line' (private, one-to-one) discussion with the offending individual.

Before giving negative feedback to a difficult person, put yourself in the shoes of the person to whom you are giving the feedback. *Negative feedback can come as a shock – how would you feel in a similar situation?* Then start with some positive reinforcement, for example, 'I'm really glad that you've been as candid with your feelings about the process as you have been.'

Giving negative feedback

Quite often a participant may be quite unaware of the effects that their behaviour is having on the rest of the group. So you will need to use a mix of sensitively chosen statements as well as questions to help any difficult participant analyse their behaviour.

Try to think through the following points:

1 **Get them to evaluate their behaviour first.** 'How do you think you're getting on with everyone else in the group?'

2 **State your feedback as a concern of yours rather than an attack on the participant.** 'I'm worried that I'm not doing a very good job of making you happier with this workshop' is better than 'You are being so critical that the group is making no progress'.

3 **Cite examples as evidence** to back up the point that you are making. It's much better to be able to talk about a couple of specific phrases or incidents rather than to make generalised statements that the participant may not necessarily understand.

4 **Check that the participant agrees with your observations.** Sometimes, the feedback may be a complete shock to the participant. Or they may not have realised that their behaviour was affecting the other participants.

5 **Suggest solutions rather than just highlight the problems.** Make suggestions such as, 'Rather than talking so much, perhaps you could . . .' or 'Perhaps you could take some of the aggression out of the tone of your voice when you do disagree with James.'

As a last resort, ask a difficult person to leave the group

Remember that your ultimate aim as the facilitator is to help the group to achieve their objectives. There may be rare occasions when it would be better to remove one difficult person from the group rather than jeopardise the efforts of all of the other participants.

Before asking the person to leave, you could first ask the rest of the group – quite publicly – what to do with the difficult individual. You should only have to ask a participant to leave when all of your other efforts have failed.

In such circumstances, you should phrase your request to the difficult participant as an option or an invitation. So you are not telling them that they *must* leave, you are asking them whether they would *like* to leave. You could say, for instance, 'I get the sense that you really do not want to be here. If you have better things to be doing, would you prefer to leave us to it?'.

You as the facilitator do not need to have all the answers

There may be occasions when the group challenges your authority. Especially when they are discussing a technically complicated topic, they may argue that you don't know anything about the topic of discussion and therefore have no right to be facilitating the session.

You really do not have to be an expert on the topic of the discussion. Instead, remind the group that, as the facilitator, you are there to:

♦ Keep the discussion moving and on track.
♦ Ensure that ideas are fully thought through.

- Act as devil's advocate and challenge the group's thinking.
- Help the group to resolve any conflicts as effectively as possible.
- Be a completely independent facilitator, with no agenda of your own to push.

If, in planning to run a workshop or meeting, you suspect that any of the participants may challenge your authority, can you get your project sponsor to come along at the start of the workshop to introduce you and give his or her implicit stamp of approval?

Be aware of external pressures that can affect your workshop

A workshop is supposed to be an opportunity for a group to take time out to discuss a topic or issue thoroughly, away from the day-to-day hassles and other distractions that could prevent them from coming up with a good solution. In reality, though, those day-to-day pressures can often intrude into your workshop. Perhaps a crisis has happened back at the office, or maybe a major customer has phoned up with an urgent request.

So what should you do?

Sticking to your planned process may well go against the best interests of the group – and it may also give you a reputation for being an obsessive, controlling facilitator too. So you might change the original objectives of the workshop. If the participants really want to talk about something different in light of external events, you could let them spend the time doing so.

Or, you could end the workshop immediately to allow the participants to deal with the crisis. But get their agreement that you will all meet up at a later date to finish off the discussion.

In summary . . .

♦ **Don't intervene too quickly when disagreements arise.**

♦ **But do take action when you are sure that the conflict is disrupting other participants.**

♦ **Use 'off-line' discussions to target particularly difficult participants.**

♦ **Give an obstinately difficult person the option of quitting the group.**

♦ **There is no need to get defensive when participants challenge your authority. Remember the value that you add by facilitating the discussion.**

♦ **Be flexible with your process and style of facilitation at all times. Sticking rigidly to your process is in no one's best interests.**

Chapter 9

Building Up Your Repertoire of Tools and Techniques

In this chapter:

- **Cause and Effect Diagram**
- **understanding Force Field Analysis**
- **using Force Field Analysis**
- **action planning**
- **six Thinking Hats**
- **working with a co-facilitator**

We have already covered some of the most common tools and techniques in Chapter 5, but having more tools and techniques in your range will really help you out. For a start, it saves you from having to reinvent the wheel each time you are preparing to run a workshop. Why design something from scratch when some of the tools and techniques in this chapter have been tested over and over again by other facilitators?

It is also important to *keep your workshops fresh and constantly engaging* for your participants. You could facilitate workshops for the same group of participants, yet still keep them on their toes by using different tools and techniques.

Having a greater variety of tools will also further build your reputation as an expert facilitator.

Cause and Effect Diagram: tackle causes, not symptoms

Let's just consider a hypothetical medical scenario for a moment. A patient goes to see her doctor and explains that she has a headache. The doctor prescribes her a course of painkillers for the symptom. Unfortunately, two months later the patient is dead – because she actually had a brain tumour that needed surgery.

The lesson behind this slightly morbid tale is that *it is dangerous to tackle presenting symptoms (i.e. the initial effects) without trying to understand the underlying causes.*

In the context of facilitation, many groups dive straight in to tackle the symptoms of a problem, without spending enough time thinking about the underlying causes. The Cause and Effect Diagram tries to separate out underlying causes from the presenting symptoms or effects.

So how do you create a Cause and Effect Diagram?

1 Identify the presenting symptom – for example, it might be poor sales of a product or low morale in the team.

2 Ask the group what causes the problem: 'Why is it a problem?' and 'What causes or contributes to it?'.
3 Write any responses that you get on a flip chart.
4 Then look at the response and ask, 'Why is it a problem?' and 'What might cause it?' to each subsequent problem that you get.

Note that each time you ask about a problem, there can be more than one cause. So your diagram could quickly get quite large.

Cause and Effect example

Consider a management committee that is looking at why their new product did very poorly in the shops:

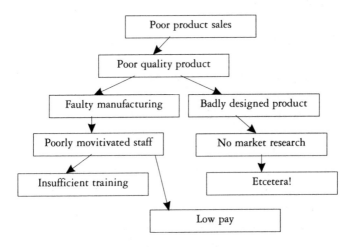

In this instance the presenting problem was poor sales of a new product. But, by digging under the surface of the symptom, we have established that factors such as insufficient training of the manufacturing operators, as well as low pay and a lack of market research, all contributed to why the product failed.

So the group can now discuss how to tackle those underlying causes rather than just the initial effect.

This tool comes under several guises. It is sometimes also called Root Cause Analysis as well as the Fishbone Diagram (because the resulting diagram can sometimes resemble a fishbone). So don't be confused if your participants use these different names for what is, more or less, the same tool.

Force Field Analysis: overcome barriers to success

The Force Field Analysis tool allows you to focus a group's attention on *how it can make change happen*. It gets its name because it looks at the driving or 'helping' forces that can make change happen, as well as the restraining or 'hindering' forces that can prevent it.

However, these forces must be helping or hindering *something*. And that something is your goal situation (sometimes also called your 'ideal situation' or 'vision'). The Force Field Analysis aims to help a group to identify how to reduce the hindering forces and strengthen the helping forces to bring about that goal situation.

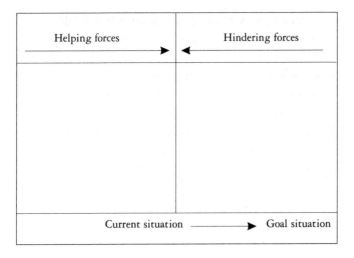

Applying Force Field Analysis

When you are preparing to do a Force Field Analysis, it is a good idea to draw the diagram up on a sheet of flip chart paper beforehand.

Then follow this step-by-step guide for using the Force Field Analysis:

1 Identify the group's goal situation. Just as a couple of examples, your participants may want to achieve a 15% reduction in departmental costs. Or perhaps they want to make the company's culture more supportive and less competitive. It will be most beneficial to your group if you can help them to describe the goal situation in as much detail as possible to ensure that everyone has a common understanding of exactly what the goals are.

2 Identify the current situation. For the most part, your participants should have a good idea of what is happening at the moment. Identifying the current situation again gives the group a common understanding of what is going wrong or not happening at the moment.

3 Explain that you are trying to push the current situation towards the goal situation (and hence the arrow connecting the current situation to the goal situation).

4 Then start to brainstorm forces that will help to move the current situation to the goal situation (i.e. forces that push the situation from left to right). You might ask a question such as: 'What actions could we take to push the current situation towards our goal situation?'.

5 Then brainstorm forces that could hinder the shift from the current situation to the goal situation (i.e. forces that push the situation back from right to left) – 'What problems might hinder or prevent us from achieving our goal situation?'.

6 As a final step, look at each of the hindering forces. Now that you have identified all of the potential hindering forces, what further actions could be taken to overcome them? Then list these under the left-hand helping forces column.

Once you have identified all of the forces that are helping or hindering efforts to bring about the goal situation, your group can think about actions that will ensure the goal situation is achieved.

Tips for analysing forces

Force Field Analysis is a good tool to use when considering how to actually change a situation. However, many participants do find this a slightly confusing tool to understand – if it is not explained clearly to them. So you must leave plenty of time in your process to explain the four key components of the analysis:

1 The goal situation.
2 The current situation.
3 Then the helping forces.
4 And the hindering forces.

Also, think about variations on how you could run a Force Field Analysis, perhaps to promote more discussion amongst participants or to introduce a change of pace into your workshop. For example, you could:

♦ Split the group into two syndicate groups to work on the helping and hindering forces separately.
♦ Ask your participants to work individually for a short period of time, writing ideas up on Post-It notes. Then get the group to share the Post-Its and look for common themes and duplication.

Turn hazy ideas into concrete plans of action

It's all very well to come up with lots of ideas during a workshop. But it can be very frustrating when those ideas fail to be translated into activities that make a difference 'back in the real world' outside of the workshop.

One of the main reasons for such failures is a lack of planning and thinking about how those good ideas will be implemented. So, action planning is a good way of helping groups to think about the specifics of how ideas should be executed. Hopefully then, by thinking about those specifics, the plan should be more easily achieved.

Action planning is a good tool to use after a SWOT, PEST or Force Field Analysis. For example, your Force Field Analysis may have identified some vague helping forces – the action planning tool can then turn them into more concrete activities to bring about change.

There are many different forms to action plans. Here's just one:

What needs to be achieved?	How will it be achieved?	What resources do we need?	Who will do this?	When will it be done by?

Step-by-step action planning

1 Draw the table up on a sheet of flip chart paper.

2 Take the first of the ideas that the group has come up with, and write it in the left hand column.

3 Then fill out each of the other columns, from left to right. For the second column, ask the group to think about the action in more detail. The idea is that, by coming up with more detail, the group is more likely to uncover obstacles and therefore think about how to avoid or overcome them.

4 Ask the group to think about resources for the third column. Remember that these are not just limited to financial resources but also materials, information, support from other people, training and technology.

5 For the fourth column, try to get a participant to volunteer to take the action on. 'Who would like to take this task on?' If the best person for the task is not in the room, perhaps a participant could at least volunteer to ask that person whether they would like to get involved.

6 Finally, get the group to think about the timescale – when the task will get done by.

7 Then go back to the next idea and turn it into a fully-fledged action plan too.

Six Thinking Hats

The Six Thinking Hats is a tool for discussing the impact of a course of action. Its creator, Edward de Bono, observed that a lot of time and energy is often wasted by having participants disagreeing with each other all the time. Typically, one participant might be arguing the advantages of one option while, at the same time, another is arguing its disadvantages.

De Bono suggested that it would be more productive to have both of these individuals thinking about the advantages at the same time, before asking them both to think equally about the disadvantages. So at no stage is there any disagreement between participants.

This technique gets participants focused in a particular direction by encouraging the participants to wear a number of different (metaphorical) hats during a discussion. These hats have been given colours, to help people remember them, and each has different meanings:

- **White hat – information gathering.** What are the established facts and figures (if any)? So no conjecture is allowed.
- **Black hat – logical, negative thinking.** What could go wrong? What are the risks, disadvantages or downsides of the idea that is being discussed?
- **Yellow hat – speculative, positive thinking.** What is good about the course of action? What are the likely benefits and opportunities?
- **Red hat – emotional thinking.** How do people feel about this? What would the impact of this course of action be on customers, employees and other people?
- **Green hat – creative, free association thinking.** This is an opportunity to think about 'pie in the sky' possibilities. If everything went 110% to plan,

what could happen? What other implications does it have for everyone involved?

♦ **Blue – organisation.** This is the hat that you 'wear' first in order to discuss the order in which the group will tackle the other hats.

Don't worry if it isn't quite clear yet how to use this tool – read on . . .

Making Six Thinking Hats work for you

If you have a group that needs to discuss a topic, begin by writing the six hats and their meanings on a flip chart (always write the blue hat up last). Divide the total time that you have to discuss the topic into six equal slots. So, if you have three hours in total, you would have half-an-hour for each hat.

Then explain briefly about the meaning of each of the hats. When you get to the blue hat, explain that you would now like the group to decide the running order of the other five hats. It's often a good idea to gather the information first, 'wearing' the white hat. But then, would they rather talk about the positive side (yellow hat) or negative side (black hat) first? Or perhaps would they rather talk about how people feel about it?

When the participants have agreed on a running order for the other five hats, ask the participants to brainstorm ideas that are in keeping with the intention of each particular hat. Facilitate to ensure that everyone follows the 'rules'. So, no negative thinking is allowed apart from during the black hat slot and no one is allowed to talk about how they feel apart from during the red hat slot.

The Six Thinking Hats can be a bit confusing for some participants. And *you do need to facilitate strongly to ensure that the participants follow the spirit of each hat*. But try it – most participants find it an unusual and engaging new way to discuss issues.

Work with a co-facilitator to make it all easier on you

This last idea isn't a tool that you can draw up on a flip chart at all. If you can find someone with whom you like working, they can help to take the pressure off you.

If you are running a workshop for several days, it can be very tiring for you to be up on your feet, talking, thinking of challenging questions and dealing with conflict for eight hours at a time. Working with a co-facilitator allows you to take a break without slowing the process down for the participants.

You can also use your co-facilitator to back you up on difficult issues. Perhaps if a group does not understand your explanation for something, your co-facilitator could try to explain it in a slightly different way.

Having a co-facilitator also means that you can run sessions in parallel to each other. For example, if you split the main group into two syndicate groups, both you and your co-facilitator could observe and facilitate each of those smaller groups.

Pitfalls of co-facilitation

However, look out that you:

♦ Make sure that you set up the tables and chairs to allow space for you or your co-facilitator to sit down when the other person is facilitating. Are you going to sit amongst the group, or perhaps at a separate table at the back or front of the room?
♦ Set some ground rules with your co-facilitator before you begin the workshop. If, for example, you are facilitating and your co-facilitator wants to make a comment, is it okay for them to do so? Or would you rather not be interrupted?
♦ Establish what role you or your co-facilitator can play when either of you is not facilitating. For example, you could help to stick flip chart sheets up on the wall. Or you could be observing the group dynamic – how the group is behaving towards each other and feeling about the content of the discussion and the process – to compare notes later on during the day. And should the other person act as a scribe or taker of minutes?
♦ Make sure that you and your co-facilitator know exactly which sections of the overall workshop process you are each going to do. Avoid embarrassing disputes in front of the participants.

In summary . . .

♦ Use the Cause and Effect Diagram to identify underlying causes rather than waste time tackling the initially presenting symptoms.

♦ Use the Force Field Analysis to understand how to bring about change.

♦ Do take time to explain the Force Field Analysis carefully – as not everyone has come across it before.

♦ Devise action plans to ensure that good ideas do not get wasted.

♦ Use Six Thinking Hats to evaluate all of the possible implications of a particular course of action.

♦ Work with a co-facilitator to make life easier on yourself.

♦ Take time beforehand to talk about exactly how you will work with your co-facilitator.

Chapter 10

Making Decisions

In this chapter:

♦ **understanding pros and cons**

♦ **casting votes**

♦ **using a Prioritisation Matrix**

♦ **ranking options**

♦ **employing a 'sanity check'**

♦ **should I use a decision-making tool at all?**

A discussion can often throw up several, if not dozens, of ideas. But the purpose of a workshop is often to identify a course of action to follow, not just options to think about.

So you may need to help the group to whittle down those many ideas into the one (or few) that will be taken forward. Sometimes, just asking, 'which is the best option?' may be enough to kick off a debate that will do the whittling for you.

When time is running short, though, it can be useful to have *a decision-making tool to help the group prioritise and focus on the few critical ideas* that it wants to pursue.

Identify pros and cons before making up your minds

Participants can often be very wedded to the ideas that they personally came up with. They are more likely to point out the advantages of their ideas or options and the disadvantages of other participants' ideas.

One way to help the group to evaluate ideas is to do a thorough analysis of the merits and demerits of each option:

♦ Simply list each idea or option on a separate piece of flip chart paper.
♦ And then ask the group to brainstorm the pros and cons of each option.

When the group has finished brainstorming the pros and cons of each one, it may become more readily apparent that a few of the ideas are not as good as some of the others – and those not-so-good ones can then be dropped.

Casting votes can help eliminate options

Voting is a rather more formal way of making a decision. A lot of participants don't like to vote because it seems to go against the spirit of openly discussing ideas and getting collective buy-in to the decision. On the other hand, *voting can save a lot of time*.

However, you must first get the group to agree how the voting will work. Will the option that gets the most votes win and be chosen? Or will the vote be used to choose the top three options for further discussion? Or perhaps a top four, five, or more? Another issue is whether you, the facilitator, should have a vote or not – especially when you have a vested interest in the outcome, perhaps when you are facilitating your own colleagues.

Whatever rules the group chooses to work with, you must check that every single participant agrees to abide by them. There's no point casting votes if certain members of the group are simply going to disagree with the decision after the votes have been counted.

Types of voting

There are broadly two types of voting:

1 **Open voting.** Simply ask each person in turn to call out his or her choice. Then, when everyone has voted, you add up the votes to announce the 'winning' option or options.
2 **Closed voting/secret ballot.** This is particularly useful when the issue may be politically sensitive, or, there may be a very senior or dominating person in the room whose vote could sway others unfairly. In such cases, you could ask the participants to write their choices down on a piece of paper.

Prioritisation Matrix: understanding effort versus impact

This matrix is simply a two-by-two grid to help the group weigh up different ideas against each other on two criteria: **effort** and **impact**.

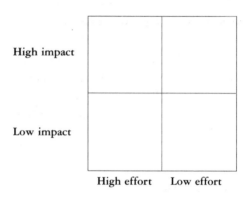

Using the grid is very straightforward:

♦ Draw the grid on a sheet of flip chart paper.
♦ Then take each of the ideas that the group has come up with and ask the participants to think about the amount of effort that it would take to execute that idea. Would it take a lot of effort (energy, time, money) or relatively little?
♦ Then ask the group to consider whether the impact of executing that idea would be large or small. However, you may need to help the group to define 'impact'. Will you use numerical measures such as revenue, profit, or growth in market share? Or would other measures such as benefits to the

environment or employee satisfaction be more relevant?

Once the group has assigned all of the actions to the matrix, the ones to focus on are obviously the ones in the top right-hand box – activities that are low effort but high impact.

Ranking can help you choose between options

Another quick way to choose a smaller number of ideas is to get the group to rank them.

You could give each participant three votes – one vote for each one of their three favourite ideas. When you have gone around the group, simply add up the number of votes that each idea has received, and re-write the ideas in a rank order from most to least popular.

If you have plenty of time, you could put each idea on a Post-It note and then ask the group to move the Post-Its into a rank order, with the most popular idea at the top and the least liked idea at the bottom. As the facilitator, you should keep asking the participants questions to stimulate their thinking and help them weigh up each of the options. Once a rank order has been decided, you will need to help the group decide where to cut off the list.

Sticky dots

This interactive version of the ranking exercise involves giving each participant a small number of adhesive stickers to put up against each idea. When the participants have all put up their 'sticky dots', you then add up the number of sticky dots against each option and re-write the list in a rank order starting with the option that had the most dots.

If you don't have any adhesive stickers (and, these days, most facilitators choose not to use them because it can seem a bit childish), you could simply ask the participants to get up on their feet and put a tick against each of their favoured ideas.

Don't be forced into decisions by your decision-making tool

The tools in this chapter are aids to decision-making. As such, they should be used to *help* a group come to a decision, not force them into accepting a decision that no one buys into. Sometimes a group may be able to reach a conclusion without the need for any decision-making tool at all.

If you do use a decision-making tool, it can be a good idea to check that everyone in the group feels comfortable with the final decision that came out of the tool. Some facilitators call this a '**sanity check**'.

There is no exact science to doing a sanity check, but some good questions to ask might include:

- 'What do we think of our final decision? Does it feel right?'
- 'Do we all agree that this is the best option(s)?'

If any of the participants disagree strongly with the decision, you may need to facilitate some discussion to get the participants who agree with it to persuade the minority of participants who do not.

In summary . . .

- **Use decision-making tools to help your group prioritise ideas and actions.**

- **Use pros and cons because it is the least artificial tool for getting a group to decide amongst options.**

- **When time is short, introduce voting as a method for making decisions about which idea(s) or option(s) to follow through.**

- **Make use of the Prioritisation Matrix to consider costs against benefits of different ideas.**

- **Or use ranking to compare the relative merits of every single idea.**

- **Run a sanity check to ensure that the decision-making tool doesn't force through a decision with which no one would otherwise agree.**

Chapter 11

Leading Your Group Over the Finish Line

In this chapter:

♦ **checking progress along the way**

♦ **parking issues**

♦ **how can I tell if it's all going wrong?**

♦ **devising contingency plans**

♦ **guiding a group to consensus**

♦ **wrapping up a workshop**

Facilitating a workshop can be an engaging and valuable way of helping a group to discuss a topic and agree how to take things forwards.

However all sorts of things can (and often do) go wrong. Participants can get stuck in heated arguments that go round and round in circles. They could rebel against the entire process that you have designed. Or they might even pretend to agree with each other just to get the workshop over and done with.

This chapter is about trouble-shooting. What can you do if you are faced with such problems?

Check progress by referring back to your objectives

Before running a workshop, a good facilitator will have designed a process with time slots for each part of the overall workshop or meeting. You may, for example, have set an agenda that allocates half-an-hour for brainstorming ideas, followed by an hour to discuss and prioritise the best ideas, before finally agreeing next steps and writing an action plan in the last hour.

So far so good.

Unfortunately, participants can often get into arguments, side discussions and debates that threaten to overrun the allocated time slots. The risk is that your participants may blame you for not managing the time properly. In such situations, you have two options. You could let the discussion/debate continue in the hope that it will produce something useful. Or you could manage the time by intervening and trying to move the discussion on.

Tips for moving a discussion on

♦ Refer back to the objectives for the workshop. 'The discussion seems to be going around in circles and I'm not sure that we are actually still discussing our original objective, which was to . . .'
♦ Apologise for interrupting. 'I'm sorry to interrupt the discussion, but . . .'

♦ Phrase your intervention in terms of not wanting to waste the participants' time unnecessarily. For example, 'I hate to interrupt, but I'm conscious that we only have a few hours to discuss the four problem areas, and we're only still on the first one.'

Managing the time

The golden rule about time is to *finish on time*. If you need to overrun by a few minutes or a quarter-of-an-hour, you can probably get away with simply apologising and thanking the participants for their patience.

If you need much more time to finish the workshop though, you must get the agreement of the participants to do so. Otherwise they could become irritated by your poor time-keeping, sending their enthusiasm and productivity on a downwards spiral.

Use 'park sheets' to keep the discussion on track

Another warning sign to look out for is when the discussion seems to wander away from the objectives. Even though the participants may have agreed on a particular set of objectives earlier in the course of a workshop, they are only human and will talk about anything that interests them.

Sometimes they may be talking about something that you would rather they didn't talk about until later in your workshop. For example, you might be running a

SWOT analysis, asking the group to talk for half-an-hour about strengths, before moving on to weaknesses for half-an-hour, and so on. But what if someone starts pointing out threats and gets fixated on them while the rest of the group are still talking about strengths?

When participants want to talk about something that they feel is more important than what you want them to discuss, the '**park sheet**' can be a tool for controlling the main thrust of the conversation.

Put a sheet of flip chart paper up on a wall and write across it the words 'park sheet'. Explain that you will use it to 'park' issues to talk about them later on in the day. By doing so, you are acknowledging their points, but simply saying that you want to talk about them at a more appropriate stage in the workshop.

Be ready to act on common danger signs

Workshops, focus groups and meetings can go wrong for all sorts of reasons. As you are running your workshop, try to keep some of the following points in mind:

1 Are the participants saying that the workshop is **unnecessary and actually a waste of time**? If they are, you need to find out why. For example, the situation may have changed or resolved itself since the group originally enlisted your help to run the workshop. If so, you may decide to put a halt to the

workshop. Your workshop, or meeting is only there as a means to an ends – it is not an end in itself.

2 Is there a **lack of enthusiasm about the workshop**? Again, it might be that the objectives for the workshop are wrong – perhaps because the situation has changed since you last spoke to the participants or sponsor. If so, how could you help the group to set objectives that are more important, urgent or relevant?

3 Is the group **struggling or failing to come up with very good ideas?** If so, are the participants the right people for discussing the issues at hand? Do they have the necessary skills, experience, or knowledge to tackle these topics? If not, how can you sensitively suggest changing the members of the group?

Have a plan up your sleeve when things go horribly wrong

The same tool or technique can have dramatically different effects on different groups. One group may, for example, find it easy to brainstorm and happily spend an hour coming up with hundreds of ideas for tackling a problem, while another might struggle to come up with even a couple of dozen.

When your process is not going down well with a group – perhaps they don't like it or just do not understand it very well – you may need to change the process.

It is therefore a good idea to have invested some time thinking about back-up or **contingency plans**. For each slot, activity, tool or technique in your workshop, spend a few minutes thinking about the following questions:

♦ What's the worst that could happen when you suggest this tool or technique to the group?
♦ And if the worst happens, what will you do? What is your 'plan B'?
♦ If you need to change this part of your overall workshop, how will it affect the overall flow of exercises later on in the workshop?

Consensus is necessary to avoid later recriminations or regrets

Disagreement during a workshop can only be good – it allows participants to challenge each other's bad ideas or poor decisions. But, at the end of the day, you are looking to get all of the participants to agree on actions or next steps that they will commit to as a result of the workshop.

In order to help a group reach consensus, you should:

♦ Allow plenty of time in your process for the participants to discuss different options and weigh them up against each other.
♦ Focus on facts rather than opinions. Facts should have more weight than speculation or unfounded opinions.

- Establish exactly what the causes of disagreements are – 'What specific parts of this course of action do you disagree with?'.
- Help the participants to negotiate with each other. 'Peter, if Isabella makes this concession, would you be willing to abide with this course of action?'.

If the group really cannot reach consensus on the issue, would it make more sense to set up another meeting or workshop to discuss it further?

Beware of false consensus

There are dangers, however, in pushing too hard for consensus. Yes, it is your job to help the group achieve consensus, but if you focus on it too much you could risk bullying members of the group into accepting the majority decision.

So you need to check that none of the participants are just going along with the rest of the group to avoid further disagreements. Firstly, remind the group that it is okay to disagree. Then ask questions such as:

- 'Is every single person happy with this course of action?'
- 'Do you all agree that this is the next step?'
- 'Would it be fair to say that you are all willing to work with this solution?'

You could also play the devil's advocate by posing an alternative argument and then encouraging the group to agree with you. For example, 'I just want to check that this really is the best way forward. What if I said that the solution you've agreed upon will never work? Can anyone think of a reason why that might be the case?'

Alternatively use a secret ballot voting process as an anonymous check that everyone really does agree with what appears to be the group's decision.

Close your workshop on a high note

Workshops can be tiring and demanding experiences for participants so it's important that you do not just let it fizzle out.

Consequently you should:

♦ **Celebrate the successes of the workshop.**
  Summarise the extent to which the group has met each one of the objectives. For example, 'Our primary objective was to decide whether to invest in this new project or not. As a result of our discussions, we now all agree that we should put together a project team along with £50,000 to pursue it further.'

♦ **Ask volunteers to type up flip chart sheets.**
  Participants often want to have a note of the ideas and suggestions that were raised during the day. Ask for a volunteer to type up any flip chart sheets and distribute them to get them to take further ownership of the commitments from the workshop.

◆ **Thank the participants for their time and efforts.** If the discussion has been very open and honest, also thank them for having been so candid with you and each other. And if you have particularly enjoyed the workshop, let the group know that too.

In summary . . .

◆ Keep an eye on the time to ensure that the group reaches all of its objectives.

◆ Use 'park sheets' to set aside issues that may only peripherally be to do with meeting the objectives of the workshop.

◆ Think about what could go wrong during a workshop – because it often will.

◆ Consensus ensures that the group's collective efforts will be focused in the same direction.

◆ Be careful not to allow a false consensus to take over.

◆ Bring the workshop to a close by focusing on the achievements of the group.

Chapter 12

Taking Facilitation to the Next Level

In this chapter:

♦ **following up on commitments**

♦ **performing a post-mortem**

♦ **enhancing your facilitation skills**

♦ **filling out the facilitation skills questionnaire**

♦ **still more tools and techniques!**

♦ **using other resources**

It is the end of the workshop and the participants have left for the day. However, your responsibilities are not over yet. There may be odds and ends that need finishing off – perhaps a report to write up, actions to complete, or feedback to give back to the workshop's sponsor.

Then you owe it to both your future groups and yourself to think about what went well or badly – and then what you could do to improve your facilitation style.

Don't forget to follow up on your commitments

When the post-workshop dust has settled, you may find yourself left with a small number of tasks to complete.

Typical activities include having to:

- **Prepare a report for your sponsor.** You may be running a series of workshops or focus groups, in which case you may wish to give an overview of the results across all of the workshops rather than the detail about each individual one.
- **Encourage networking between the participants.** Sometimes the participants may want to stay in touch with each other, perhaps for networking purposes. If that's the case you could get all of their contact details (email addresses, telephone numbers, addresses, etc) and distribute these to the group.
- **Follow up on any actions** that you have agreed to take on. In particular, if you were facilitating a team that you belong to, you may have accumulated some responsibilities as a result of the discussion.

'Buddying'

On occasion you may want the group to stay in touch with each other – perhaps after a training workshop where you want the participants to review new skills with each other. Some tips for setting up 'buddying' or peer coaching:

♦ Ask the participants to get together in pairs. Alternatively, you could suggest pair groupings – for example to put two participants together who have considerably more or less experience than the rest of the group.

♦ Suggest a rough agenda of what each pair needs to do when they get together. For instance, if you had run a workshop on a new set of skills, you might suggest that they discuss a set of questions such as: 'Have you tried your new skills?', 'What do you still need help with?', etc. The idea is that each participant's 'buddy' can listen, make suggestions and act as a sounding board.

♦ Then suggest some guidelines for how each pair should work together. For instance, you may want to suggest how often they get together, and how long they meet for.

♦ Do check that the participants are happy with your guidelines. For instance, it's better to have less frequent meetings that the pairs will actually attend, rather than trying to enforce more frequent meetings that they would simply ignore instead.

Gather feedback to gauge your performance

After all the effort of designing and then running the workshop, isn't it natural to hope that the workshop will be a success? As a result, it can sometimes be easy for facilitators to delude themselves about the success of a particular workshop after the event.

A less subjective measure of gauging the effectiveness of the workshop is to ask the participants. You could speak to the individual participants to ask their opinions. You could ask them:

1 What was good about the workshop?
2 What was bad about the workshop?
3 What would you suggest doing to improve the workshop?

Using feedback forms

If you are running a one-off workshop, you could type up and hand out an anonymous feedback or 'post-mortem' form. Very simply, it could just be a single side of A4 with the three questions above and blank spaces for the participants to scribble their thoughts.

If you want a better sense of what was good or bad, you could include scoring scales. For example, you could ask questions that start along the lines of, 'On a scale of 1 to 10 (where 1 = worst you've experienced to 10 = best you've experienced), how would you rate . . . ?'

When you hand the forms out do stress that the feedback is anonymous, because only then will you get the most honest feedback.

Other forms of feedback

You really cannot get too much feedback. Two other ways of getting feedback are to:

1 Get feedback from your co-facilitator. Before a workshop, ask a colleague to observe your facilitation and take a few notes on your performance. After the workshop is over, the two of you can sit down and debrief on what was good or not so good.
2 Record your performance on video. Watching yourself on video can be excruciating, but invaluable. In particular, look at your posture and body language. Watch your hands too – do you wring them, put them in your pockets or flap them? Do you speak loudly enough for all of the participants to hear? And do you make eye contact with every participant as opposed to fixing eye contact only on one or two people?

Facilitation is a skill you need to work at

We have already talked about the three elements of good facilitation – process, content and group dynamics (back in Chapter 1). Many people have a tendency to neglect one or even two of these elements. So when you've spent some time facilitating, it's worth checking that you are paying equal attention to each element.

For example, some people are strong at guiding a group through a process, but might pay less attention to whether the group are buying into the content or not. Or a facilitator who focuses too much on making sure that the group dynamic and mood are good may allow the process to spiral away, meaning that it could take eight hours what it should have taken four to accomplish!

Have a look at the following quiz. It will help you to identify your areas of relative strength as well as where you might be weaker and need development. Just answer 'yes', 'sometimes', or 'no' to each question.

Fill out the facilitation skills questionnaire

With regards to the **process** of the workshop, do you always . . .

1 Know who is coming to the workshop, and also their job titles and a bit about them?
2 Make contact with the participants before the meeting to research and build rapport?
3 Explain the background and set the scene at the start of the meeting?
4 Explain the objectives?
5 Check that the participants agree with the objectives?
6 Explain any process that you might use?
7 Manage the time effectively?

Thinking about the **content**, do you always . . .

8 Hold your own views back?

9 Avoid getting sucked into the content by deflecting questions back at the participants?

10 Present information that is relevant to the discussion?

11 Challenge irrelevant debate?

12 Ask questions that move the discussion along?

13 Achieve results as compared with the original objectives for the workshop?

Finally, on the **group dynamics**, do you always . . .

14 Break the ice between participants at the start of the meeting?

15 Make eye contact with every participant in the group?

16 Ensure that both quieter and louder participants have an equal say in the discussion?

17 Manage conflict between participants?

18 Check that the group has reached true consensus?

19 Close the workshop on a high note?

Now that you've gone through the questions, ask yourself: What could you be doing better?

Just five more tools and techniques

We're almost done with this book, but I thought I would leave you with a quick handful of other tools and techniques that you could use as a basis for stimulating discussion – all of which have handy acronyms by which to remember them. These can be a useful checklist to act as a reminder to talk about certain issues during a meeting or workshop.

Do bear in mind that these are not set in stone – so make sure that you adapt them to fit the needs of each of your individual groups.

Marketing mix – four Ps

This framework may be useful when your group is trying to figure out how to launch a new product or service.

The four 'P's of marketing are:

1 **Product** – what are the goods or services? Issues include product features, quality and reliability. How will it be installed, serviced and maintained to offer customer satisfaction?
2 **Price** – how much will the product cost? And what about discounts for bulk purchase?
3 **Place** – how will the product be distributed or made available to customers?
4 **Promotion** – how will the product be communicated to customers, using methods such as advertising, public relations and point-of-sales activities?

By using this framework for questions, you should be able to come up with a more thought-through action plan.

Three Cs of business strategy

This framework is used to help a group discuss how to develop a business strategy. The three 'C's are:

1 **Customers** – who are the paying customers or clients? How will your strategy affect them?
2 **Competitors** – who are your present competitors? If your strategy takes you into new arenas, who will be your future competitors? And how could they undermine your strategy?
3 **Corporation/company** – what factors within your company need to be taken into account? This could include factors such as the company's management, culture, assets and capabilities.

Using the three 'C's can again help your participants to think through some of the risks of any business strategy they put together.

MOST

Another acronym! This one stands for:

♦ **Mission** – an organisation's (or team's or division's) purpose and direction.
♦ **Objectives** – the organisation's long-term goals.
♦ **Strategies** – the long-term plans to achieve the mission and objectives. These tend to be more conceptual and focus on a one- or two-year timeframe.
♦ **Tactics** – short-term plans for achieving those strategies. These tactics tend to be more detailed

and may describe month-by-month or even day-to-day tasks and activities.

This acronym is a way for a group to think about an organisation's purpose and how to turn an idea into practical actions.

Organisation design – seven Ss

The seven 'S's serve as a prompt to think about certain factors about an organisation when considering how to make change happen. They are as follows:

1 **Structure** – what does the organisation chart for the company look like? Or what would it look like after the change?
2 **Strategies** – how does the organisation plan to achieve its goals?
3 **Systems** – what processes or technologies need to be considered?
4 **Shared values** – what (if any) are the principles and beliefs that guide people in this organisation? And what should they be in the future?
5 **Style** – what is the culture of the organisation? How does it need to change?
6 **Staff** – what kinds of people need to be involved? Do new employees have to be recruited?
7 **Skills** – what skills do employees have? And what skills will they need?

There's more to facilitation than just this book!

This book has:

♦ Established the principles of facilitation.
♦ Introduced some basic tools and techniques commonly employed by facilitators.
♦ Suggested methods to keep participants engaged and interested in what's going on.
♦ Raised your awareness of ways for dealing with conflict and difficult people in order to achieve the group's objectives.

However, this book can serve only to whet your appetite for facilitation. If that's the case, what other resources can you draw upon?

Books

Hundreds of new books are published every year on facilitation, handling meetings more effectively, injecting creativity into workshops and so on. A couple of 'classic' books include:

Serious Creativity, Edward de Bono (Penguin, 1985). De Bono is widely regarded as an expert in tools and techniques for encouraging creativity.

Games Trainers Play, John Newstrom and Edward Scannell (McGraw-Hill, 1980). Filled with exercises and activities that get participants talking with each other. There are also follow-up volumes imaginatively titled *More Games* . . . and *Even More Games* . . . However, select carefully which exercises are appropriate for each of your particular groups.

Email

If you need help send an email message to me, Rob Yeung, at the following email address: *robyeung@robyeung.freeserve.co.uk*

Good luck!

In summary . . .

♦ Follow up on your commitments to ensure the discussions during the workshop are not wasted.

♦ Gather ongoing feedback from participants to gauge their perceptions of your facilitation skills.

♦ Do also take time to evaluate your own performance.

♦ Keep learning about facilitation – reading and networking will take you a long way to finding out about other exercises, tools, techniques and methods for getting results from facilitation.